Reviewers' cor

Cold River Spirits

✧ ✧ ✧

"Those who wish to understand how complicated, difficult, and painful it can be to cross the divide between cultures should not miss the key Jan Harper-Haines offers in COLD RIVER SPIRITS. Her memories of her Athabascan-Irish family's struggle to escape hopeless poverty in Alaska's Yukon valley is told with wit and skill showing the humor and joy as well as the sorrow of the struggle. But its greatest importance lies in the understanding it offers."
    Tony Hillerman, author of HUNTING BADGER

"COLD RIVER SPIRITS is about struggle, fortitude, and hope."
    Ronald Spatz, Editor, ALASKA QUARTERLY REVIEW

"COLD RIVER SPIRITS is an important link to the long and tumultuous history of Alaskan Natives that needed telling . . . "
    Velma Wallis, author of TWO OLD WOMEN

"This book provides sensational snapshots of a land and life unimaginable to modern readers with remarkable immediacy: the arctic air's chill tickled my nose hairs, I heard the Nicolina's cackle, and smelled the heavy aroma of roasting bear meat . . . "
    Mary Westheimer, BOOKZONE.COM

"I couldn't put the book down until I had read every word and then wanted to know more about this remarkable family."
    Helen J. Ibach, LONE PINE PUBLISHING

Cold River Spirits

Whispers from a
Family's Forgotten Past

Jan Harper-Haines

EPICENTER PRESS

Epicenter Press is a regional press publishing nonfiction books about the arts, history, environment, and diverse cultures and lifestyles of Alaska and the Pacific Northwest.

Publisher: Kent Sturgis
Acquisitions Editor: Lael Morgan
Editor: Kathleen McCoy
Map: Marge Mueller, Gray Mouse Graphics
Proofreader: Sherrill Carlson
Cover & text design: Elizabeth Watson, Watson Graphics

Library of Congress Control Number: 00134933
ISBN 978-1-935347-15-6

10 9 8 7 6 5 4 3 2 1
Printed in the United States of America

COLD RIVER SPIRITS was published previously in a hardbound First Edition from Epicenter Press in 2000.

To order single copies of this title, mail $14.95 plus $6 for shipping and handling (WA residents add $1.90 state sales tax) to Epicenter Press, PO Box 82368, Kenmore, WA 98028; call us day or night at 800-950-6663, or visit www.EpicenterPress.com.

 Find us on
Facebook

Photographs supplied by the author are from the Harper family collection unless otherwise credited.

PHOTO CREDITS:
The Anchorage Museum at Rasmuson Center: page 133
Archives, Alaska and Polar Regions Department, Rasmuson Library, University of Alaska Fairbanks: pages 6, 25 (Accession number 897-2n), page 41 (The Stephen Foster Album, Accession number 69-92-777), page 65 (further details unavailable), page 67 (Drane Album 2, page 51, Accession number 91-046-531), page 71 (The P.S. Hunt Album, Accession number 80-68-421), page 73 (The Stephen Foster Album, Accession number 69-92-489), page 100 (The Baker Collection, Accession number 88-196-13), page 119 Accession number 58-1026-1998), page 129 (The Fred Machentaye Collection, Accession number 73-75-157), page 137 (The Dorothy Pattison Collection, Accession number 86-094-34).
Candy Waugaman Collection: pages 3, 6, 8-9, 13, 21, 39, 43, 47, 57, 59, 89, 95, 192 (Larry Petri).
Archives of the Episcopal Church USA: pages 21, 35, 68.
National Archives and Records Administration: page 93
Yvonne Mozee: page 172

COVER PHOTOS: Front, Flora Jane Harper as a young woman in Tanana; back cover, sisters Connie, Elsie, and Flora Jane Harper in Fairbanks; Louise Minook Harper and her two sons, John and Arthur, in Fairbanks.

In memory of
Louise Minook Harper,
who called the wind,
and
Flora Jane Harper Petri,
who wanted this story told.

The Episcopal Mission in Tanana

Jenny Harper

Louise, Martha, and children

John and Martha Minook

FAMILY

		Esther	Joyce		
		Richard	Ronald		
	Jan Petri	Phyllis	Edward	Johanna	
	|	|	|	|	
Hilda	**Flora Jane**	**Elsie**	**Arthur**	**John**	**Francis**
B. *Unknown*	B. 1910	B. 1912	B. 1914	B. 1916	B. 1918
D.*Died within*	D.1992	D.1982	D.1989	D.1996	D.1972
days of birth					

Also:

Lucy

Fannie

Andrew

Adam

Elizabeth

Joseph

Louise Minook

B. October 1892 Tanana

D. July 1968 Fairbanks   MARRIED

Russian and Athabascan
John Minook
(Pavloff)
B. 1853 Nulato (Alaska)
D. 1939

Athabascan
Martha Sport
(Yawhodelne)

TREE

Louise and Sam

	Nichole			
	Diane			
	Kathleen			
	Ella	Dana		
	Steven	Max		
	James	Debra		
	Sherry	Mary Elizabeth		
Anna-Louise	Julie	Robert		
Tom	Susan	Bruce		
Maxine	Michael	Lloyd	Robin	
|	|	|	|	
Connie	**Weese** **Walter**	**Mary**	**Don**	
B. 1920	B. 1922 B.1924	B.1928	B.1930	
D.2011	D.1996 D.2005		D.2011	

Also:
Andrew
Alfred

1907   **Samuel Harper**   Frederick
B. October. 1884 Tanana   Charles
D. November 1931 Fairbanks   Walter
Marianne
Margaret

Irish   *Athabascan*
Arthur Harper   **Jenny**
B. 1835 Ireland   (Seentaána)
D. 1887 California   B. 1856
D. 1932

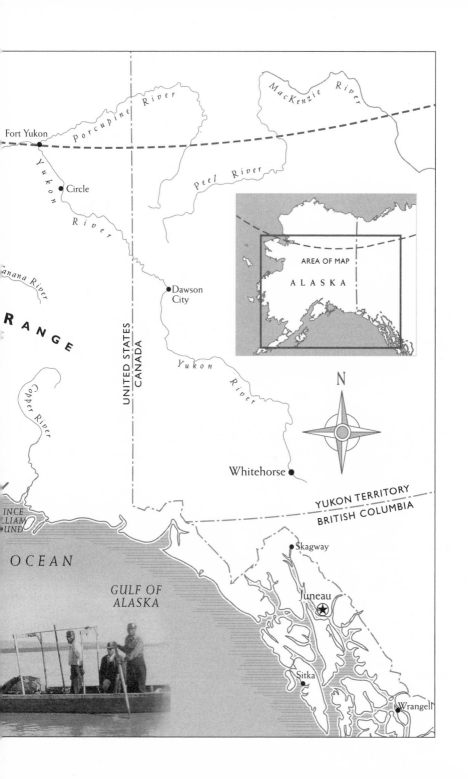

Porcupine River

MacKenzie River

Fort Yukon

Yukon River

Circle

Peel River

Tanana River

RANGE

Copper River

UNITED STATES
CANADA

Dawson
City

Yukon River

AREA OF MAP
ALASKA

N

Whitehorse

YUKON TERRITORY
BRITISH COLUMBIA

PRINCE
WILLIAM
SOUND

OCEAN

GULF OF
ALASKA

Skagway

Juneau
★

Sitka

Wrangell

Louise Harper (left), her sister-in-law Martha Minook, and children

Acknowledgments

I began this book in 1990 with writing classes at College of Marin. Generous souls supported and critiqued my efforts. My gratitude to Jackie Kudler, Betty Hodson, Mike Carter, Regula Noetzzli, Judith Nies, Deborah Atkinson, Dale Schnell, Kathy Paddock, Ralph Gabrielli, Maxine Felice, Max and Georgia Lou Johnson, Jane Evanson, Andrea Simpson, Christopher Myrdal and Catherine Shelburne.

I applaud the staff at the San Anselmo Library and the University of Alaska Library. The chamber of commerce and tourist bureaus at Tanana, Nenana, and Rampart, Alaska provided much-needed maps and local history. I happily browsed through the ample photo collection of Rampart at the Fairbanks *Baan O Yeel Kon* office.

I applaud the staff at the San Anselmo Library, and at the University of Alaska library and archives, where I pored through books and photographs. The Chamber of Commerce and Tourist Bureaus at Tanana, Nenana, and Rampart provided much needed maps and local history. At the Fairbanks *Baan O Yeel Kon* office, I browsed through their photo collection of Rampart.

Jim Voden of the Water Division for the State of Alaska in Fairbanks cheerfully provided me with maps and historical information on the Chena River floods.

Mary Denton, Connie Paddock, Angela Harper, Don Harper and John Harper, Ethel Pronesti, Richard Fast, Esther Fast, Clara Johnson, Sally Hudson, Mike and Jane Harper, Maxine Richert, Yvonne Mozee, Ella Blair, and the late Louise Blair and Louise Davis provided me with photographs and information I could have gotten no other way. My thanks to Hazel Knox Pilkington who began researching our family tree 30 years ago—and to Prof. Phyllis Fast who completed it.

My gratitude to linguist Dr. Eliza Jones and her daughter, Susan Paskvan, for their help in translating the robin's song my mother sang in Koyukon. Thanks also to CIRI, who awarded me a grant in 1995.

Lael Morgan, a saint in disguise, and familiar with the Harper family from her knowledge of Alaska history, called me on New Year's Eve in 1996 with suggestions on organizing the material into a book. I had been looking for this kind of help for two years. I am indebted to her and to Kent Sturgis at Epicenter Press for their encouragement and the work they've put in on this. Lael's advice, to have fun, boosted me through when the going got muddy. My thanks to Darryl Lundahl for his help on so many levels.

Above all, my husband's support, feedback, and belief in the Harper story made it possible to write about this unique family.

*The author's mother, Flora Jane Harper, was the
first Alaskan Native to graduate from the University of Alaska.*

Table of Contents

Spring flooding on the Tanana River.

Jan Harper-Haines as a child with her mother, Flora Jane, and father, Walter "Pete" Petri.

Prologue

I was three years old when we lived in Sitka, and I came home one day with the announcement, "I'm not going to play with those kids—they're Indians!" Dad raised his eyebrows and my mother disappeared into the kitchen. Then Dad sat me down and told me I was half-Indian. I was shocked. He went on to tell me how special Indian children were and how lucky I was to have an Indian mother.

Years later, I was surprised when I overheard Mom call herself ordinary. Eventually, I realized ordinary was what she wished for, to be like everyone else. "In my next life," she said, "I want to be a blonde with fat legs—mine are so skinny!"

❖ ❖ ❖

My mother began telling Dad and me about her childhood when I was very young. She told us about her family living along the Yukon—in Rampart, Nenana, Tanana—and later in Fairbanks, Eklutna, Wrangell, and Anchorage. Sometimes mysterious, sometimes frightening, never ordinary, these stories told of the Chemawa Institute in Oregon where her desperately poor father sent his four oldest children for ten years for their education (mainly, so they'd have food). They told of my mother's struggle with tuberculosis and poverty as she worked her way through college. As I grew older, she'd add, "Someone ought to write these down." Her dark eyes were on me, her only child.

In 1990, after seventeen years in advertising and marketing financial institutions, I took a writing class. The fiction classes were full; the only opening was in a class called Tales Told from Memory. It didn't sound exciting, but writing was writing, and I had to start somewhere. The first assignment was to write a character study.

One night I was reading in bed and something made me look up. Grandma was sitting in front of me. She wore a brown print dress, a hand crocheted sweater, thick hose, and heavy brown oxfords. Her church and travel outfit. Her opal ring shimmered. She was gazing to her left. I blinked and she was gone.

The next day, I began a character study of my grandmother. As the assignments graduated to full-blown essays, I wrote my mother's stories and discovered my grandmother at the heart of each, whether in fact or spirit. Gaps were filled in with phone calls and letters to my mother, aunts, and uncles. "Oh did you know . . . ?" Aunt Mary began, when I called with some innocuous question. From that phone call I wrote Ice Fog about a startling situation my grandmother found herself in, but one my mother never mentioned.

15

COLD RIVER SPIRITS

Mary Harper Denton (left) with her niece Jan Harper-Haines

Jan, her grandmother Louise, and mother Flora Jane

❖ ❖ ❖

In 1935 my mother was the first Alaska Native to graduate from the University of Alaska in Fairbanks. Her uncle, Walter Harper, had been the first to reach the top of Mount McKinley in 1913 and his father, Arthur Harper, was among the first to discover gold on the Yukon. My mother's other grandfather, John Minook, was the first to find gold in the Rampart area. His discovery attracted thousands of stampeders and built the town of Rampart.

Flora Jane and Jan   Pete and Jan

Through the centuries, those who lived along the Yukon learned ways to heal themselves with the help of nature. They knew ways to protect themselves from danger. They understood that making love under the Aurora Borealis, when nocturnal lights thrummed the sky, could result in the birth of a special child—one who was a bright light to the Dena, the people.

They never said aloud the name of one who had died for fear of summoning that spirit. They tried to avoid bragging about good luck, knowing they'd lose it if they did. They honored nature and her spirit world. If they forgot, and bad luck started following them like a slavering wolf, they knew why.

They knew when something unusual happened in nature, something bad was coming to the Dena. They knew when they died their spirits would return to the headwaters of the Yukon, as their ancestors had promised. A special few could interpret dreams. For others dreams came true. This book was my mother's dream.

❖ ❖ ❖

I discovered in talking with relatives that oral history changes with each storyteller. Reflections of some situations and incidents in COLD RIVER SPIRITS, a work of creative nonfiction, may conflict with how others remember them.

Indian Ways

✧ ✧ ✧

My mother never drifted far from the spirit stories of
her childhood, but she also talked about her father, Sam,
and mentioned children appearing along the trail where he
delivered mail by dog sled—children who looked so much
like Sam that people joked about it.

She told us how my grandmother Louise, at age five,
found the grocer shot and bloodied in his store. "Go away
little girl, go away!" he hissed, waving his hand as if to
push her out the door.

My grandmother's life seemed to lurch from one unusual
and difficult situation to another, brought on by spirits,
teasing Nicolina, or Sam's infidelity.

1

Flood on the Chena

Spring floods were practically an annual occurence in Fairbanks.

When the Chena River overflowed its banks in 1948, as it did nearly every spring, Fairbanks took on the appearance of a slowly moving lake. The dirty brown water, dotted with chunks of ice, logs, carcasses of dead animals, and other debris from the long winter, spread across the little river town.

Lapping steadily, the floodwater crossed First Avenue and crept up the steps of the Episcopal Church and into the Masonic Temple. It leisurely entered saloons on Second and filled stores and houses all the way down Barnette Street past Seventh.

On Garden Island, the water hesitated at the steps of the Alaska Railroad depot like a mannerly aunt unsure of her welcome. A moment later, it washed across the old plank floor, covered the benches along the walls, and reached the top of the ticket counter.

The river rose fourteen feet as it flowed into truck stop cafes and smoky dives where the only women were bleary-eyed hoostitutes.

The water appeared smooth, even languid, but its rapid undercurrents and eddies swirled with energy. The force was enough to carry away sections of wooden sidewalk and cave in cellar doors all over town. With no hesitation it entered Louise Minook Harper's log cabin on Fifth, five blocks from the river.

A drunk wading home from the bars on Second stumbled on a washed out section of sidewalk and was swept into the river where he smacked his head on a passing log. His body was found a few days later, tangled in the flotsam of a floating tree.

That morning two other men died in a fight in the Nevada Bar over the timing of the Chena breakup. A third man, clutching the winning ice pool ticket, suffered a black eye and cracked his false teeth in the commotion. When two officers from the Territorial Police arrived, big and blustery in their uniforms, the survivor convinced them the two men had stabbed one another. This stretch of truth was heartily supported by the bartender and other none too sober patrons.

When the river receded a few days later, flood-weary residents reclaimed their homes and took stock of the damage. Whites, Natives, hoostitutes, and prominent families dragged muddied books, ruined mattresses, and unrecognizable whatall into the street to be hauled away.

❖ ❖ ❖

The sour stench of mildew, river sludge, and dog poop gagged Louise when she opened the shed door. *"Chanh na banh!"* she swore, turning her head and blinking as she propped open the door with a shovel and stood outside while the cramped space aired.

Her glance fell on Sam's trunk in the corner. It was slimy with mud.

Holding her breath, Louise grabbed the cracked leather handle. The muck made a sucking noise as she pulled the trunk from the shed. Inside, Sam's papers and notebooks squished at her touch. His penciled words were blurred, and those written in ink were a blue smear. Louise glimpsed the butt of a pistol wedged into one side of the trunk.

She looked around her small, muddy yard. Her house was already full of damp clothes, smelly rugs, and bedding. There was no place to dry the trunk's contents. On top of that, the stove was filled with silt. The electricity was out and they still had no drinking water.

❖ ❖ ❖

"The trunk is gone? Dad's stories are gone?" Flora Jane tightened her lips to keep them from quivering. Louise glanced at her oldest daughter and sighed.

"Everything was wet, it was all ruined." Louise was making a piecrust, and she took her black mood out on it, smacking the rolling pin, pushing the dough around.

Ever since she'd had George haul the trunk to the street, she'd been answering for it. Even George had looked perplexed and said, "Are you sure?" Louise whacked the rolling pin again on the flattened dough. Flora Jane glanced at Elsie. The crust would be tough as a boot.

"Your father sent his stories to that Hollywood movie man, Sam Goldwyn. One was a finalist, is that what you call it? A 'finalist?'"

Flora Jane nodded. She had never heard the Sam Goldwyn part before.

"Then he got a letter back." Louise unfolded the dough. "It said the stories would be better if they were typed." She snorted. "Can you see a typewriter hanging off the side of the sled, along with food, kids, and everything else?"

Her daughters laughed, their eyes on the pie. Weese, Connie, Elsie, and Flora Jane had gathered at the little place on Fifth to help their mother clean up. Mary was still at work.

"Hey, Mom, remember how Ethel Milligan used to call you Louisie?" Connie laughed. "You really let her have it!"

"Mom sure got on her high horse when kids weren't respectful enough," Flora Jane added. "You were always reminding us how your great grandfather, Pavloff, was the first Russian commander at Fort Nulato. And how Dad's father, Arthur Harper discovered gold on the Yukon."

"Don't let Sally Mayo hear you—Cap Mayo and Jack McQuesten were right there with him," Louise said, smiling.

Pride in her family had kept Louise going, especially when Sam was off doing who knows what and she was left alone with the children.

Louise finished the pie, shoved it in the oven and sank into a chair with a virtuous sigh. Now, if she could only have a drink. But Flora Jane was there, and her eldest daughter worried about her health. That meant her drinking. Louise glanced at the clock. She could wait.

"Where'd this come from, Mom?" Connie fingered the scarred pearl handle of the small pistol. Louise had been unwilling to toss it out with the ruined trunk. She glanced at the rusty gun.

"That belonged to my sister, Lucy," Louise said. "From when she and Howard shot the grocer in Tanana."

Louise's older sister, Lucy, left home with her
Native boyfriend at age 14.

2

Lucy and The Gun

John and Martha Minook (right) had seven children, including Louise.

Lucy's mukluks slipped on a patch of ice and she went down hard, landing on her hip. *"Dad tsen tsiegha!"* she hissed hoping to ward off evil spirits who might take advantage of her fall. Cushioned by a long skirt, long underwear, and parka, she scrambled unhurt to her feet. Sweat trickled down her back as she trotted on in the darkness. The gun pulled heavily in her pocket.

Light from a waning moon filtered through the trees and shadows streaked across the snow. Up ahead, the dark shape of the Minook cabin appeared. As she approached the clearing, where the dogs were tied to stumps, she slowed to a walk. "Prince, King . . . stay!" Her voice was low. Watching her, their noses twitching, the huskies settled down without barking.

Don't let the door squeak, she prayed as she pulled and slightly lifted it, managing to muffle the sound. From a shelf inside, she removed a glass shade from a kerosene lamp and lit the wick, keeping it low. An aroma of stew and the pungent odors of freshly tanned furs filled the small cabin. From behind a hanging blanket she heard her mother's low breathing and her father's rattling snores. Shielding the faint light with her body, Lucy made her way to her younger sister's bed.

Louise was five and a light sleeper. Nestled under a caribou hide and blanket, she heard the faint creak of the door. Then she felt the bed sink. In the flickering light, Lucy's face was hidden behind the wolf ruff of her parka. Her breath had dampened the guard hairs of the ruff, and she shrugged the hood back, her black hair spilling out. Her rounded forehead, small chin, and full lips flashed in the lamp's shadowy glow. Clouds of icy air rolled off her parka. Louise shivered as she struggled to sit up.

"Hide this for me, don't let anyone see it!" Lucy whispered. She pushed a small, dark object across the caribou hide. Yellow light shimmered off the pearl handle. Louise stared at the gun, then looked at her sister. In the shadows, Lucy's eyes were invisible.

"I'm not marrying that man," Lucy muttered.

Their father had promised Lucy to the wealthy owner of the general store, a white man. The marriage could benefit the entire family, depending on the man's generosity. But to Lucy, age fourteen, the forty-five-year-old man seemed ancient. Besides, she was in love with Howard, a tall Athabascan boy.

To Lucy's father, Howard wasn't worth thinking about. "He's a half-breed! You want to have lots of children, be poor?" Ignoring his daughter's stubborn expression, Minook had ranted on. "You marry a white man—a rich white man!"

Minook spoke from experience. With no knowledge of birth control, Natives often had huge families, too many to feed when fishing and hunting were poor and traplines were empty. Minook and his wife Martha knew this too well. Four of their eight children had died of illnesses worsened by hunger. White families seemed to have fewer children and plenty of food. Minook wanted a better life for his daughters, even if it meant marrying them off to white men.

With her tiny waist, thick, black hair, and dark eyes, Lucy was the third of four daughters, two of whom had died young. "Shaped like an hour glass," the grocer bragged to his friends. Neither he nor Lucy's father thought twice about Howard, Lucy's Native boyfriend. After all, women were taught to obey their fathers and husbands.

Not Lucy. When she and Howard entered the store late one night, they knew the older man would be alone, most likely drinking, as he did every night while restocking his shelves and working on accounts. In the shadowy darkness, his hand wobbling, Howard lifted the gun, aimed, and pulled the trigger. The surprised grocer, who hadn't seen them enter, let out a squawk and fell heavily against a shelf, toppling it with a clatter. Canned goods crashed and rolled on the floor as his beefy legs slid in front of him and his head and shoulders came to rest against a wooden pickle keg.

The noise and blood shocked the young couple. They only wanted to scare the white man from marrying Lucy. Nearly wetting themselves in fear, they stumbled outside. Now they had no choice, they'd have to leave Tanana.

Revived by the cold air, Lucy took the gun and started for home while Howard made his way to the Yukon River to find his brother's boat. Minutes later, Lucy joined him and they began the cold trip downriver. They'd have to figure out a way to board a sternwheeler for St. Michael's, and from there a steamship to Seattle. None of this had they planned. It just happened.

The next morning, when Martha Minook discovered Lucy's undisturbed bed, she felt a flutter of panic. Had her daughter run off with Howard? The agitated woman needed time to think, and she did her best thinking alone. Under the guise of baking a pie, she hustled Louise off to the store for apples.

When the five-year-old girl pushed open the heavy door of the general store, she blinked in the unexpected darkness. By now the shades should have been raised and the lamps lit. Peering through the gloom, Louise saw a bulky shape on the floor.

In the hours since he had been shot, the grocer's blood had stained the planks beneath him. When the door banged shut behind her, the semi-conscious man blinked. In his delirium, he imagined the gunman was still there.

"Go away, little girl!" he hissed, his breathing labored. "Get way!"

Alarmed, Louise backed away as the man looked around. Daylight flashed again as she pushed open the door, revealing the cashbox, still intact. Relieved, the grocer sank back.

Louise was red-faced from running when she tore into the house. "The grocer's sleeping on the floor and there's blood," she blurted. Martha gaped at her breathless daughter, then hurriedly pulled on her mukluks and parka.

❖ ❖ ❖

"Probably someone wanting to rob me," the grocer muttered as Martha Minook cleaned and bound his wound with strips of an old dress. But she suspected differently. She hoped if Lucy was gone, she was gone for a long time.

Andrew, Sam, and Fred Harper
were sent to California for school.

3

Sam and Louise

Louise Minook, 15, married Samuel Harper in 1909.

When Arthur Harper's five sons returned to Tanana from school in California, "they never knew what hit them," relatives agreed. Their mother *Seentaana*, or Jenny as her husband called her, was Athabascan and wanted her children with her, but the boys and their two sisters were sent away one by one when they turned five.

Their father, an educated man from County Antrim, Ireland, recognized that the missionary schools were little more than orphanages. When one child got sick, they all did, sometimes perishing by the score. Against Jenny's wishes, he sent his children to California for their schooling. Arthur Harper was well off but, when one of his partners embezzled money from their lumber mill in Circle City, Harper's sons had to quit school and return home. The two girls stayed to earn teaching degrees from San Francisco Teachers College.

Village life in Alaska stunned the boys. Accustomed to electric lights, flush toilets, and heat at the touch of a switch, they were plunged into a tiny settlement with no electricity or plumbing. Kerosene lamps and candles provided weak, flickering light. Outhouses and "going" in the bushes—or in the front yard, in the case of children—were common. Families slept close together in one room, even as couples enjoyed one another under wriggling blankets and hides.

Most Natives spoke one of several Athabascan dialects—none of which could the Harper sons understand. The young men shared a small cabin with their mother. It reeked of cooking odors, tanning solution, hides, and other parts of dead animals. Heat poured forth unevenly from a stove made from a fifty-gallon drum with a makeshift pipe poking through the roof.

Walter, the youngest, the special child Jenny managed to keep with her, was raised in Native ways. He could find safety in a whiteout and coerce the most cantankerous dogs into pulling a sled. He was skilled in tracking, trapping, fishing, and starting a fire in any weather. Archdeacon Stuck at the Tanana Mission School was so impressed by Walter's manners, intelligence, and skill in handling dogs that he took a special interest guiding the boy's studies.

◇ ◇ ◇

OK, so what if Louise Minook, at thirteen, was in love with Walter, with his beautiful Irish-Indian face, his easy smile, his quick wit? Everyone in Tanana knew that Stuck had plans for Walter, for his education, and for climbing Denali. And all the girls in the village knew those plans didn't include marriage.

When Sam returned to Tanana from California, Louise already knew about him and his brothers from Walter. Sam was good looking and soon all the girls were eyeing him. Louise was fascinated by him—he could read and write and talk about things that had nothing to do with hunting, fishing, trapping, the weather, building a smokehouse, or dogs. She herself knew little of life outside the village, and could neither read nor write, but she knew from her father that education was important. After losing his gold claim to the Americans for being "too Russian," John Minook had taught himself to read, write, and speak English.

Events between Sam and Louise might not have proceeded so rapidly if John Minook hadn't come home drunk one night with a white man. It was the end of September, two weeks before Louise turned fourteen.

Louise was now as curvy and feminine as her sister, Lucy. Black haired, jet

Walter Harper was raised in Native ways.

eyed, and round faced with flawless brown skin, Louise stood just five feet tall. The evening her father stumbled home with the stranger, she was sorting laundry and ironing. The white man was so filthy his face looked gray and his clothes were stiff with grime. From the sour smell of him, he hadn't bathed in months. Louise's mother was chopping moose meat and she turned her face away. *Kuyh!*

Breathing cautiously through her mouth, Louise shoved the table toward the window where the draft was icy, but fresh. Table legs screeched over the floor, but the men, sitting on crates, paid no attention as they passed a whiskey bottle back and forth.

"Found a nugget big as that fry pan," said the white man, Harold. Frowning with sincerity, he hiccuped. The black cast-iron frying pan on the stove was burbling with moose meat, carrots, potatoes, and wild celery.

"You didn't!" John Minook reared back on his crate and stared at the pan as if it could talk.

"Did!" The stranger nodded, solemnly. The aroma of Martha Minook's stew filled the cabin and his stomach growled.

Louise's sadiron had a metal plate that clamped to a handle. There were more such plates hanging from the stove, and she replaced the one she was using.

"Harold's got a gold mine," Minook said, suddenly. He gave the women a triumphant look. The white man's shoulders straightened and his rheumy eyes clung to Louise's blooming figure like sap on a tree.

"Staked my claim 'fore anyone else . . . no one'd been up that part of the crick." In the foggy hollows of his memory, Harold recalled Natives were contemptuous of boasting. Unless it was their own, of course. "I got lucky," he added, but the flush-faced girl and her mother were now blowing their noses and fanning the air around them.

Harold's avid interest in Louise had not escaped her father. Carefully, so as not to fall over, Minook leaned toward his new friend and began whispering in his dusty ear. After several moments, Minook reared up, nearly falling off his crate. "Louise," he bellowed. "Harold here's going to be your husband."

Louise looked up from ironing and blinked at her father. After a moment, Harold gingerly pushed himself to his feet. As he spread his arms in happy lust, and lurched toward the surprised girl, Louise tightened her grip and swung. The heavy sadiron made a flat thumping sound, and the miner flew back and crashed to the floor, bright blood gushing from his dusty nose and whiskered chin. After a moment, John Minook got to his feet and peered down at his friend. The iron had left an imprint on his face.

Forcing herself to move, Martha grabbed a wet cloth, and hurried to the prone miner. The rag, none too clean to begin with, turned pink and grimy as she cleaned his face. Her thoughts roiling, she prayed he wouldn't remember. He was out cold and very drunk, maybe he'd believe her if she told him he'd fallen and hit his head.

That night Louise crept out of the house as her parents slept and the bandaged miner's snores filled the air. Ten minutes later, she found Sam at the cabin he shared with his older brothers. In hurried whispers, they borrowed a sled and two dogs from his brother, Charlie. By early morning, Sam and thirteen-year-old Louise were on their way across the snow pack.

They lived in the bush for a year before returning to Tanana.

✧ ✧ ✧

Before the arrival of Christianity, Indian marriages were simple affairs. Using a stone ax, the man would chop a couple of month's supply of wood for the woman's parents. The job was difficult and it took days. Then the marriage was announced at a potlatch or to the village at large. All this changed with the arrival of a new Episcopal priest.

"You need to be married in a church to make it legal and proper in the eyes of God," he told Sam and Louise, his black robes swinging heavily. Louise had never seen anyone so impressive.

The day of the ceremony, she wore a long plaid dress she had gotten from the mission and altered to fit. Her black hair was coiled on top of her head and she appeared taller. Sam was dignified and handsome in a brown suit and crisp white shirt. Louise had beaded his moccasins in a blue fleur-de-lis and they peeked out from his pant cuffs.

When John Minook learned of the wedding, he ranted, "That half-breed! Now she'll have lots of children. Those Harpers were raised white, what do they know about how we live?"

Martha raised her eyebrows at her half-Russian husband. "Why are you calling him a half-breed?"

"Because that's what he is!"

"Well, what do you think I married," she snapped.

✧ ✧ ✧

There was so little food their first winters together that Louise's monthly time stopped. When she was fifteen and they were back living in Tanana, she had rabbits from her trap line, Sam had shot a moose, and fish were plentiful. A year later when her monthly time disappeared again Louise was so busy she barely noticed.

Must be an upset stomach, she thought as she brewed spruce tea. Spruce was good for almost everything. The feeling continued, and she went to her mother. "When did you have your last bleeding?" Martha asked, peering at her pale, sweaty daughter. Louise shook her head, she didn't remember.

By this time Lucy had returned to Alaska, arriving in Tanana with a white miner from Montana named Sven, and a baby daughter, Catherine. Now twenty-five, and eleven years older than when she and Howard had shot the owner of the general store, Lucy still had an hour-glass figure. Her makeup, styled hair, and clothes—in fashions more often seen on white women—had men from Tanana to Seattle turning for a second look.

"I thought we'd never get to Seattle," Lucy told her younger sister. She and the pregnant Louise were picking berries near Fort Gibbon in Tanana and keeping an eye out for bears. "When we finally got on the boat at St. Michael, a storm came up and the boiler went out, and there was talk we might have to turn back."

When Lucy and Howard reached Seattle, Howard struggled to find work. Finally a man offered him a laborer's job at Port Angeles on the other side of Puget Sound. From the first day, Howard found himself the target of white men who spit in his path and called him a "dirty half-breed." Howard tried to ignore them, knowing if he fought, he'd get the bejesus beat out of him. As the days passed, he often found himself stopping at a saloon after work. As he drank, he grew morose.

Now pregnant, Lucy often felt sick at the mere smell of food. One night, she told Howard she felt too ill to cook. To Howard her ill-timed words were the final insult. She started to say something else when his fist shot at her. Hot blood filled her mouth and she fell against the stove. Howard hit her again, this time above the bridge of her nose, knocking her into the wood box with such force her head snapped and she chipped a tooth.

"Stop it, you sonofabitch!" Lucy screamed at him, blood gushing from her mouth and nose. Weaving slightly, Howard stumbled outside, the door slamming behind him.

Lucy closed her eyes and sank back on the rag-rug she had finished only the week before. Her two front teeth were loose, and the chipped tooth sawed at her cheek. When a jagged pain tore through her belly, she whimpered and rolled onto her side. After a moment, wetness seeped through her bloomers. Tugging at her skirt, Lucy felt inside her thighs. Her hand came away stained with blood. It was too soon.

"I'm telling you, Louisie," Lucy said, as she popped a blueberry into her mouth. "Was I ever glad we didn't get married. After that, I wasn't about to stay with that *Changh!*"

❖ ❖ ❖

After three days of labor, Louise was drenched in sweat, even though snow was on the ground and the cabin was drafty. "Harder, push harder," Lucy ordered. Alternately squatting, then resting on her back with her knees up, Louise looked away from Lucy's tiny waist. Just the thought of a corset was unbearable. Another spasm ripped through her, and with a cry she pushed.

"It's coming!" Lucy's voice rose. "It's coming! I see it!" With another shove, Louise felt her first baby emerge.

"I have it," Lucy shouted. "A girl! You have a girl!"

4

Hilda

Women pack gear into a birch bark canoe.

A bright gray sky hung over the river like a huge bowl, and their voices floated up into it and disappeared. With the put-put of the cranky outboard motor and the cold river air whistling past their ears, Sam and Louise gave up trying to talk. Together two years, they headed for one of their summer campsites to cut wood for the big sternwheelers that traveled the Yukon after breakup.

The Yukon was a mile wide in some places, gray and choppy, and the wind was brisk. Even in May, the chill in an open boat could saw through your bones.

Overhead, the caw of a raven cut through the wind and Louise looked up, squinting as the bird flew across the river. Sniffing the air, Louise detected a hint of spring, a whiff of things growing. Behind her, Sam gripped the tiller, his eyes moving constantly as he watched for floating logs and broken ice that could rip a hole in the hull. The silvery fur of his caribou parka shimmered in

35

the gray light. Underneath, he wore a sweater and shirt, denim pants over long johns, and three pairs of socks under his oiled "waterproofed" mukluks. Louise also wore layers of clothes because it was the easiest way to carry them. Hilda, the baby, two weeks old, was nestled in a birch basket and tied to Louise's back.

From the shore, Queenie and King yipped as they crashed through the brush following the skiff. Steering carefully, Sam avoided a couple of logs partly hidden beneath the ice. Louise pointed to the shore and shouted, "There, over there!" A haze obscured the beach. As they drew closer Sam recognized the rocky landing and steered toward it.

Ten feet away, he cut the power. The uneven beach rose abruptly and grated the hull as he poled to shore. Sam grabbed a rope tied to the bow and jumped into the water. As he waded, pulling the skiff, Louise heaved herself over the side. The baby on her back threw her off balance, and she went down. When she reached the beach, her skirt was soaked to her thighs and her teeth were chattering.

Sam pulled the skiff onto higher ground, and they began unloading their tent, stove, provisions and floor boards. Behind them, a gentle slope leveled off into a flat spot, ideal for a campsite. The hill behind this small plateau was forested with spruce, willow, birch, and alder. Sam pitched the tent and arranged the floorboards inside.

Sweat ran down his face as he hefted the heavy metal stove up the hill. Midway, he stopped to catch his breath. Having a stove in the camp was worth the effort, what with icy winds whistling up from the cold river. The stovepipe was lighter, and Sam soon had the sections connected and sticking out through the roof of the tent. Last, he opened an airhole flap for ventilation.

Taking a handful of raisins from the food box, Sam looked up at the hills. He wondered how he could devise a better method of moving the logs. Each year he had to go farther from the river for wood. As it was, the dogs pulled a small platform loaded with wood while he rolled bigger logs down to the river. On the beach, he cut them into four-foot lengths to fit the steamship boilers. Maybe he would build a cart that moved on wooden rails. As he thought about it, he picked up his ax.

"Queenie, King!" he yelled as he started up the hill.

While Sam pitched the tent and assembled the stove, Louise made several trips from the skiff, bringing their food, cooking utensils, and bedding. She fit a large knife into the leather sheath at her waist and with Hilda still dozing on her back, began climbing the hill behind the tent. From experience,

Louise kept to the edge of the forest. No telling if bears, wolverine, or moose were nearby.

Overhead, a raven cawed and, with a noisy flapping of wings, landed on a skinny branch in front of her. Its licorice feathers gleamed as the bird cocked its head and watched her climb the hill, a tiny head bobbing from the hump on her back, black wisps of hair showing beneath the blanket.

Louise struggled up the hill, her feet sliding over the slippery undergrowth. She remembered stories her mother and father told. How owls warned the *Dena* of death, and jays alerted hunters when moose or caribou were near. How birds carried spirits of the dying back to the headwaters of the Yukon. When a bird comes into your tent, her mother had said, you must kill it. Louise frowned. What happened if you didn't? It had been a long time since she'd heard the stories.

The woods were full of spindly spruce. When she came to a clump of evergreen, she cut off several branches, getting the sticky, brown pitch on her hands and parka. She carried the branches back to the tent and spread them on the floorboards. Indian feathers, some called these boughs specially cut for beds. As Louise worked, the fresh, pungent aroma of the spruce seemed to lift the headaches and exhaustion she'd had since Hilda's birth.

When the boughs were layered to the thickness of a mattress, she covered them with a canvas tarp, then with a moose hide, fur side up, and finally with the blankets. For pillows, she added a few more springy boughs. When the bed was finished, she kneeled onto it and loosened the baby from her back. Fear niggled at her as she braced the infant on the bed with a blanket. Hilda was so quiet compared to other babies in the village. Telling herself not to worry, Louise went outside to build a fire.

She was filling a pot with water and coffee grounds, the way Sam liked it, when he and the dogs came scrambling up the slope. "It's not ready yet," she said when her husband eyed the pot. He sighed and went into the tent. It was still too cold for mosquitoes so the flap door could stay open.

"*Gin eeydee!*" The canvas muffled the surprise in Sam's voice. Louise was trying to hang the pot over the fire, but the hook was bent wrong. "There's a *dilk' ahoo* in here!"

"A *dilk' ahoo?*" Louise stood up. "A robin?" she asked in disbelief. Dropping the pot into the fire with a clatter, she ran into the tent. Inside, a young robin was flying over the bed, trying to land on the stovepipe. Louise grabbed an old sweater and began flapping it. "Out, out!" she yelled. Dread made her legs weak.

Startled, the robin flew up and clung to the ventilation flap. Louise flung the sweater in the air again, snapping it like a flag in the wind. The young bird released the flap and fluttered to the side, barely missing the ugly green sweater. Crying now, Louise hurled herself at the bird.

"Out, out! Get out!" she screamed.

Sam was stunned by her agitation. Suddenly, the robin vanished through the airhole. Louise dropped the sweater, her shoulders sagging. Now she remembered. She should have killed it, as she had been taught. When a bird enters your house you must kill it before it's too late.

"It's just a bird, a young bird, *a saanhggaagga yoza*," Sam said in confusion.

"The baby, how's the baby?" Louise was hoarse from yelling, and her voice came out in a croak. She dropped to her knees on the bed. Hilda's skin seemed oddly blue in the afternoon light. Louise picked her up, automatically patting her bottom. The tiny body was limp. The baby's head lolled, even as Louise braced it with her hand.

"Let me have her." Sam held out his arms. Looking at his daughter's tiny face under the frowsy black hair, he frowned. She was so still. Not like herself—her eyes finding him, her fists waving.

"She's not breathing!" he whispered. Sam peered into her mouth, was something stuck? Holding her upside down, he smacked her backside. But the baby was silent. Her brown eyes, tinged with blue, were murky and unseeing.

"NO!" Sam's voice rose.

But Louise didn't hear him. All she heard was a raucous whispering. As if her head were filled with ravens. *When a bird flies into your home, it will steal someone's spirit.*

From a long way off, as if from across the river or beyond the mountains, she heard a mournful keening—an eerie, rhythmic wail.

Outside, Queenie and King pricked their ears. Lifting their heads, the huskies joined in, their voices mingling with hers.

Their cries flew to the sky and echoed off the river.

They sank like mist over the forest.

5

Sam's Women

Sam delivered mail using a dog team such as this one.

Sam and Louise were living some miles out in the bush, and one morning they decided to go to Nenana to pick up their mail and get supplies. Nenana was a river town above Fairbanks with a mostly white population and a smattering of Natives. The new Alaska Railroad would cross the Tanana River there.

When they reached the outskirts of Nenana, where they were staying with Sam's brother, Charlie, Louise went out to feed and water the dogs. Sam had gone already, hiking the half-mile or so into town.

As she fed dried fish to the huskies, she heard voices from the other side of the shed. The murmuring was indistinct so she moved closer.

"Guess he's still seeing Eliza . . . " Louise recognized the gravelly voice of Edward, one of Sam's cousins.

"*Oho,*" agreed a second male voice. Louise guessed it was Charlie. "Think she knows?"

Louise grew still. *Knows what?* Around her, the impatient dogs whined and strained toward the bucket of fish.

"Can't see her putting up with it, can you?" the first voice continued. Their mukluks crunched in the snow as they walked away.

The dogs' whining jolted Louise and she tossed them the rest of the fish.

Louise knew her husband, like his brothers, had girlfriends in the past. But did he still have them? In winter Sam and Charlie delivered mail by dog team, earning twenty dollars for each round trip. These trips took three to five days, depending on the weather, and the brothers stayed overnight with families along their routes. When a child appeared later, bearing a striking resemblance to the Harpers—the high intellectual forehead, the full mouth, the well-shaped nose—people nudged one another. "Those Harper boys!" they said, but never when Louise was nearby.

Louise saw the Harper look-alike children but she thought they were Charlie's. "Charlie should get his own woman," she told her husband. "One of those husbands is going to come home with a loaded rifle at the wrong time."

"Hmmmm," was all Sam had said.

Back in the cabin, Louise absent-mindedly put socks and moccasins on Flora Jane's feet. Louise had to admit Sam had been evasive lately. Lighthearted, even happy.

Several hours after she went bed, the door burst open, and Sam came in with a rush of cold air. As he stomped the snow from his mukluks, Louise, still awake, peered at him. He was humming bits of the *Tennessee Waltz* and smiling.

She closed her eyes. Nobody gets that silly look just going for mail and provisions.

6

The Nicolina

Approaching Rampart on the Yukon River.

It was a warm June evening after a long, exhausting day and Louise and Sam were relaxing in their tent at Twelve-Mile Island. Sam was sitting on the bed, reading a story in *Collier's* magazine to Louise and the children. As he licked his fingers to turn the page, something struck the tent with a loud thud.

"Mud ball, mud ball!" five-year-old Flora Jane yelled, pointing a sticky finger at a dark shape rolling down the tent wall. For a moment, her parents froze. Then, dropping the magazine, Sam scrambled to his feet and rushed outside, Louise right behind him.

"This way," Sam yelled as he started up the hill behind the tent. Louise sneezed as she climbed after him. In the air she thought she detected something rank, like old fish. The faint breeze shifted toward the river and, on the beach below, the huskies began whining as they picked up the strange scent.

Sam headed east, searching the ground and woods. Louise climbed in the opposite direction until she reached a cluster of trees. She glanced at the beach below and saw the grasses wave and flatten.

"Look!" she yelled. "Down there!" A large round shape covered with twigs and leaves was rolling toward the river.

Sam began side-slipping down the hill while she peered nervously into

41

the woods. The trees were skinny and the brush thick. Overhead, the sky was streaked with flame, pink, and orange, and dotted with white clouds. Louise turned back. "*Changh na haungh!*" she swore when she saw the tent. The pale canvas was streaked with mud.

Sam climbed back up the hill, panting. "It was a ball of mud . . . with a rock in the middle." He shrugged and shook his head. That evening they tried to clean the tent, but the silty mud just smeared deeper into the canvas.

The next morning, Sam pulled on his jacket and stuffed a list of supplies into his pocket. Groceries, magazines, pick up the mail.

"The sooner I leave, the sooner I'll get back," he said, avoiding the look from his unhappy wife. After last night's scare, she didn't want him to leave.

She had dressed carefully that morning in a long-sleeved white blouse and full-length blue skirt, what she wore to the monthly dances in Rampart. She didn't want her husband's last image of her to be of some poor, bedraggled squaw.

The breeze from the river was chilly and she pushed her hands into the folds of the skirt as she followed Sam to the beach. Sam shoved the skiff into the murky water and jumped aboard. Using a pole, he pushed the boat farther into the water before starting the motor. Within minutes, he disappeared into the mist rising over the river.

From the beach, Louise looked at the thick, secretive woods behind the campsite. There would be a big moon that night. Odd things happened when the moon was big. Much as she tried not to think about it, she knew this was a time when *Nicolina* were most likely to appear.

When Louise was a child, she heard how the *Nicolina* liked to tease and could scare the living daylights out of people with their eerie laughter and shrieking. How they stole food and tools and even children to raise as their own. When she was nine, she had even seen one.

"A ghost!" a white man on the dock had yelled. The villagers watched in awe as a large, man-shaped creature dashed across a mud flat. The *Nicolina* was moving so fast that it barely left a mark. From where Louise stood on the bank, the faint tracks looked like human footprints with long toenails. When a raven cawed overhead, the people on the bank laughed nervously.

The elders said that long ago when starving Indians crossed the ice following caribou herds, they'd been forced to leave behind their old, their infirm, and their deformed. Some outcasts, particularly the deformed with their large, misshapen heads and strong bodies, survived and became fast runners. "Like lightning," people said. The Natives called these creatures *Nicolina*,

Sam and Louise earned money by chopping firewood for Yukon River sternwheelers.

meaning wild man. From bears, the *Nicolina* learned to hibernate for escape from the cold of winter. From spirits, they learned to disappear at will.

Louise turned back to the river, her mukluks silent on the rocks, and began chanting in *Dena*. The dogs watched, their ears pricked. Turning now toward the hills, she prayed to the spirits of the earth. Then, looking at the sky, she remembered the mission prayer. What could it hurt? The spirits weren't jealous. "Our Father, who art in heaven," she began.

Finally, she started up the slope. Inside the tent, Flora Jane played with a sock doll while Elsie and the baby, both having eaten, were sleeping. All that day the dogs were quiet. But that night, after she and the children went to bed, the huskies started chuffing, a low, nervous *"huh, huh."*

Louise awoke instantly. She tried to think. If it were a bear, the dogs would have barked. That rank smell the day before was it a *Nicolina?* Then she heard a soft rustle of breaking twigs. It moved slowly around the tent, not lumbering like a bear, but heavier than a lynx or wolf.

Louise pushed aside the mosquito net and crept toward Flora Jane's cot. She shook her daughter. "Wake up! Wake up!" she whispered. Flora Jane groaned and opened her eyes. Next to her, Elsie and the baby stirred. Louise spotted a pie pan and large spoon and shoved them into Flora Jane's hands. Her eldest daughter pushed herself up and stared sleepily at the pan.

Louise, now thoroughly frightened, was shaking so hard she nearly

Louise, Flora Jane, and baby Art   *Flora Jane with brothers John and Art*

dropped the dishpan and spatula she'd found for herself. In the gray-orange summer light, tension tightened her face, making the young mother suddenly appear ancient. Before the frightened children could cry, Louise whacked the dishpan with the spatula. The jarring noise sent a shock wave through the still night. Outside, the dogs' whining gave way to frantic barking.

Again and again, Louise banged the dishpan. Flora Jane, her mouth open, stared at her mother.

"Go ahead, hit the pan! Make a lot of noise!" Louise yelled. Then she began to sing, "Hasn't antee botee seen Kellee?"

Flora Jane joined in, beating her pan and singing. Not to be left out, Elsie and the baby began to wail. The agitated dogs lifted their heads and howled. Louise swung into *Onward Christian Soldiers*, then *Swing Low, Sweet Chariot*, and *Amazing Grace*. Flora Jane hollered "Ya ya ya ya" when she didn't know the words. Finally, Louise sang Indian style, "*HiYA, HiYA, HiYA,*" punctuated with eagle-like screeches. The children yelled themselves hoarse.

After about twenty minutes, her ears ringing, Louise let the dishpan slide to the floor. Flora Jane also stopped beating her drum. Her throat was raw and her hands ached. "*Eenaa,*" she began.

"*Daalak!*" Louise hissed, her face intent as she listened. Finally, she turned to her daughter. "Go back to bed now, get under the mosquito net."

"When is Dad coming home?" Flora Jane asked, pulling the blanket to her chin. This was not like other nights and she wasn't sure if she should be scared.

"He'll be home in a little while." Louise put the pans into the box and climbed into bed, exhausted.

Outside, dark light reflected off the river, and wisps of clouds drifted away from the full moon. The terrible odor faded and the dogs curled themselves into balls on the rocky ground. All but Queenie. Her ears pricked, her nose twitching, she stayed alert until the moon disappeared in the gray dawn and birds began singing.

✧ ✧ ✧

It was raining when Sam returned two days later. He had been delayed by a search for the Bjorn's two-year-old son, Bobby, who had disappeared from his parents' tent upriver from Rampart.

"A lot of people were out searching the woods and river." Sam pulled off his parka and began shedding his wet clothes.

"Is he gone? Is Bobby gone?" Louise was still jumpy from the night before.

"Gone? Oh no! We found him." Sam sank onto the bed and pulled off his mukluks. They had leaked, and his feet were cold and wet. He sighed as he wiggled his wrinkled toes. "He was in the woods, way up Big Minook creek. Don't know how he got that far alone."

Sam stood and began unpacking the supplies. "Did you hear any more noises?" Sam didn't want to hear about *Nicolina*. They were just bears, he figured. Or maybe hunters who had wandered off and lost their senses. Being alone for a long time in the woods made people crazy.

Flora Jane wandered into the tent. "*Eetaa*, we sang and sang and yelled." Her voice was raspy like she had a cold. Louise spun her around and steered her back outside.

"The *Suzy* is coming," Louise said. "Watch for the boat, but don't go near the water!" The arrival of the *Suzy*, a big, white sternwheeler, was a major event. Sam raised his eyebrows. The *Suzy* wasn't due for several days.

"Everything is fine," Louise said, keeping her voice calm. The night before, she remembered something her older sister Lucy had said. Men hated to hear women complain. Louise sighed. Well, in a day or two, the big moon would pass, and the *Nicolina* would go back into the woods.

She reached for the new *Saturday Evening Post*. On the cover was a picture of a white family having a picnic on a grassy hill. A dog romped with a child, and everyone was smiling. Louise snorted to herself. With all those trees and that grass, she knew there were mosquitoes. And no telling what else.

From left, Adam Minook, his wife Martha,
and Louise holding her son Francis with
Arthur and John Harper in front.

7

Whistling for the Wind

Landing the mail at Rampart during breakup.

Flora Jane was lying on the roof enjoying the hot sun against her back when she saw two hunters prop their rifles outside the Rampart General Store and go inside. A large, gray carcass slumped next to their backpacks, and she squinted at it before deciding it was a wolf. The store was just down the hill from the Harper's house and Flora Jane had been watching it ever since her mother had gone inside several minutes earlier.

Tiyh do was a Native community on a rise above the main town of Rampart. While Natives could shop at the Rampart store for sugar, flour, and gasoline for their boats, they were not welcome to live in the largely white town. Of course, exceptions were made for white men who took Native wives. The shortage of women in Alaska deemed this a necessity.

A squeal of laughter erupted inside the house, followed by crying. With a sigh, Flora Jane crawled to the corner of the roof, climbed down, and marched into the house ready to swat whoever was to blame. Before she had a chance, her mother burst through the door, panting.

"The hunters say the blueberries are ripe!" Louise dropped a box of groceries on the table. "There's good picking, but we have to hurry or the bears will get them."

Her excitement was contagious, and Elsie and Arthur began running around the house, yelling, "We're going berry picking, berry picking!" In truth, they were more excited about the games than the berries. Secret games their mother knew, but played only when their father was away.

"I don't want our children growing up believing in superstition," Sam Harper said at the merest hint of anything unusual. Trouble was, almost everything Louise did was unusual. She had even inherited her father's ability to predict the arrival of the steamboat—when there wasn't a hint of it on the horizon. Some of her children also had this ability. At times, Flora Jane glimpsed things she later realized were not seen by everyone. She called these her "awake dreams."

After rinsing dust from the water can, Flora Jane filled it from the community well. Everyone, even the smallest child, carried something. As she tied a sack of raisins to Arthur's back, Louise said, "This way, they won't spill all over the ground when he runs and falls."

When the babies were anchored across her back in a blanket, they left the house. Other women and children clattered out of their houses to join them. At twenty-five, Louise was a midwife, and the younger women often sought her advice on child rearing and health matters.

Clouds of gnats and mosquitoes hovered in the muggy air. Despite the heat, the women wore long-sleeved shirts, long skirts, and scarves or hats swathed with mosquito netting over their black hair. Everyone wore moccasins.

Sweltering in their denim overalls and heavy shirts, Flora Jane, Elsie, and Arthur were giddy to be going someplace. Their outdoor play areas were limited. The deep, silty Yukon flowed and swirled on one side. Bears roamed the hills on the other.

Sis, or black bears, are smaller and more easily frightened than brown bears or grizzlies. They also love *geega*, berries. The *Dena* solution was to go berry picking with a half-dozen or more families including children who, for once, were encouraged to make noise. The cacophony of rocks against tin cans and children shrieking and hollering kept the shy bears away.

As she walked, Flora Jane remembered her grandfather telling her it was bad luck for women to eat or touch any part of a bear. Grandfather Minook said women antagonized a bear's spirit.

"Never eat bear meat," he'd told Flora Jane. "It will make you barren."

Only women past childbearing years were allowed to cook bear meat or to tan the hides. But when they watched the men and boys feasting on the rich meat, the women sometimes grumbled that these bear stories were a lot of hooey so the men would have the meat for themselves.

The sweet, light fragrance of dogwood and lupine hung in the air as the families climbed the hill. Bees drifted from flower to flower as if dazed by the heat. The hills that looked soft from a distance were covered with willows, birch, spruce, foxtails, devils club, shrubs of Indian tea, and blue-berry and cranberry bushes. By keeping to the narrow path, the dozen or so women and children avoided the sticky foxtails and thorny devils club.

When they reached the top, Arthur raced off to play with the Mayo children. Louise settled the babies on a blanket under a bush and draped a mosquito net over them.

"Even one *tl eeyh* (mosquito) can keep a baby awake and crying," she said, securing the net around the babies. Once or twice, she had tried to teach Flora Jane and Elsie how to pick berries properly, but the impatient girls hadn't gotten the hang of it. Now, as they crouched before a *nilyaag*, a blue-berry bush, the girls sneaked glances at their mother.

"In nature," Louise told them, "everything has a spirit. Now look at this one. . . . " she pointed to a nearby bush, "See? This one doesn't feel ready."

The girls peered at the bush. It did seem to give off an air of reluctance. Still, Flora Jane wasn't sure she'd have sensed this without her mother there to tell her.

". . . So let's see why." Louise lifted a small branch with two blueberries. The underside was a hard, unripe green.

On her knees, Flora Jane dropped blueberries into her can with a soft plop. In the distance she saw women stand to stretch the kinks out of their backs. Sitting back on her heels, she looked down at the Yukon River. Under the vivid sky, the river was blue-green.

The Yukon could appear calm but it was unpredictable. Many people had drowned after falling from boats, rafts, even fish-wheels. "You fall in there and you're lost," her mother said. The river's spirit wasn't to be tampered with by giddy children.

By afternoon, their baskets and cans were full. Louise spread out their picnic of hardtack, peanut butter, salmon strips, raisins, and tea. Soft, muffled laughter and voices floated through the still air from the other families. It was no longer necessary to make noise, as bears are known to sleep through the heat of mid-day.

Squirming with anticipation, the hungry children ate quickly. Even Flora Jane, who regarded herself as almost an adult since she took care of the others, felt her stomach flutter.

After they had eaten, Louise put her cup down and got to her feet. She picked up a blanket, flung it over a wide bush, and patted a slight hollow in the middle. She moved to one side of the blanket, waving the children to the other side. Flora Jane, Elsie, and Arthur were silent, but their senses were wildly alert.

Inhaling deeply, Louise quieted herself. After a moment, she lifted her head and uttered a single, low whistle. The clear sound pierced the heavy air. It raised the hair on the children's necks and arms. A chill ran down Flora Jane's sweaty back. Her mother paused, lifting her face, closing her eyes. Her mood of expectation was so great, the children didn't dare blink for fear of missing something.

Then she whistled the same low note. Again she paused. The still air hovered like a nesting bird. In the distance, sounds from the other families faded. Even the mosquitoes were quiet. Again Louise whistled. This time, a slightly higher note.

After a moment, Flora Jane felt her hair lift and ruffle. Leaves overhead rustled as branches swayed and dozing birds blinked. Sprightly breezes fanned the children's skin. A warm gust flipped up a corner of the blanket. Strands of black hair from the girls' braids blew against their faces. The rush of air was fragrant with Sitka roses, Balm of Gilead, and spruce. Shifting slightly to loosen her shirt, Flora Jane felt the breeze cool her sweaty arms and back.

Moving quickly, Louise tipped the first basket over the blanket. As the berries fell, gusty air currents blew away twigs, dirt, leaves, and small insects, blowing it all over the edge of the blanket. The children stared wide-eyed as she emptied basket after basket, can after can, the berries rolling into larger and larger clusters, while the winds did her bidding. Finally the last container was empty.

With the children on one side and Louise on the other, they lowered the sagging blanket to the ground. The wind died as suddenly as it had risen. Dropping to their knees, the Harpers refilled the baskets and cans. When the last container was filled, Louise sighed and sat back on her heels. Gazing across the hills at the other families, she said, "Flora Jane, run tell the others it's time to go."

Popping a ripe berry into her mouth, Flora Jane jumped to her feet.

Unlike cranberries, which tasted better cooked with sugar, blueberries were naturally sweet and had a way of disappearing before they could be made into anything. Better yet, they stained teeth and tongues blue, making berry picking even more fun with the children lunging at one other, pulling their mouths in scary blue grins.

As she raced through the brush, nearly tripping where spongy undergrowth hid thick roots and fallen branches, Flora Jane yelled to the other families, "We're going home now, we're going home!" Then she ran back to help tie the babies to her mother's back.

"Is that it, do we have everything?" Louise asked.

Dutifully, the children made a show of looking around. Then, they started down the narrow path. From her place at the rear, Flora Jane glanced back at the trees. The leaves drooped as if exhausted. Bushes and branches, waving wildly moments before, were still. Birds slept. Even the hordes of mosquitoes, gnats, and no-see-ums were quiet.

In the afternoon silence, Flora Jane remembered her Grandfather's words, "Always give thanks to the spirits."

"*Basee*," she whispered, keeping her voice low, so the others wouldn't hear. Then, feeling a surge of happiness, she shouted, "*Basee, anaa basee!*"

Sam Harper

8

Sam and Helen

The responsibilities of being a husband and father became too much for Sam.

Unlike his brother Walter, Sam Harper was likely to lead a dog team in circles if there was no trail. Until he acquired a sense of direction, Louise had to lead the team. Sam mostly worked odd jobs, all a half-breed could expect at the time. His dream was to write.

In the evenings, after the chores were done, Sam recorded the day's events: A chance encounter with a cow moose and her yearling calf. The dogfights and tangled traces when the team chased a bitch in heat. Fishing through the ice, his skin turning blue, snow yellowed with dog pee or black with soot. He described the sled's jarring vibration that ran up his legs and shook his entire body when the dogs raced over snow-covered fallen trees, stumps, and rocky outcroppings. He described the sounds of sled runners whishing through the heavy quiet of winter and the explosion when tree limbs cracked in the frozen air. The freedom he felt with sky and land unending in every direction. As if he and the dogs were at the top of the world, and nothing else existed.

Yet, responsibilities and troubles did exist. And a pattern developed. When the weight of being a husband, father, and provider became too much for him, Sam turned to drink and his old girlfriends. Ribald women who had the grace not to get pregnant. If only Louise knew the secret!

When he stayed away, he was sometimes gone for days. With so many children to care for, Louise had little choice but to ignore Sam's running around. Until one afternoon when Sam came home wafting stale odors of hootch and tobacco. He plunked himself into a chair.

"I want a divorce," he said, spreading his hands on the table. They were callused, with cracked nails, stained from working on the truck and in the garden. Louise was eating a piece of toast, and it stuck in her throat. Her eyes watered and she coughed.

"Why?" she managed.

Sam straightened, his courage enhanced by whiskey. "I'm in love with Helen Callahan." As soon as the words were out of his mouth, he wished he were sober. Taking a deep breath, he plowed ahead. "I want to marry her."

Shock, indignation, and rage flared inside Louise. Helen Callahan was an attractive, unmarried cousin. "*Changh*-bastard!" Louise hissed, her face tightening with fury. Sam braced himself.

After a moment, Louise calmed herself. "Fine," she said, her voice level.

Surprised, Sam stared at her, his face lifting with hope.

"You can have your divorce, but . . . " she paused until he looked her in the eye, "you have to take the children, too." What followed was dead silence.

Helen Callahan was no fool. She didn't want four kids not her own. Even if it meant getting Sam Harper.

9

The Knife

YUKON RIVER FISH CAMP, 1918

Flora Jane (right) and her siblings helped out at the Harper fish camp.

In the summer, the Harpers' fish-wheel brought up hundreds of fish, mostly kings and chums. Louise fixed fish everywhich way, and her salmon strips were thought to be the best on the river. "Not fatty or fly blown, like some," her children bragged.

After weeks of eating fish, however, even the best of it becomes tiresome.

So when Julia Carlo invited the Harpers over for lasagna, the family accepted eagerly.

The following Sunday, they climbed into their *baalgaas*, as Koyukons called their boats, and set out for the Carlo's fish camp. The sky was a vivid blue, the air clear, and the river a calm green-gray. White castle-shaped clouds drifted overhead while robins and sparrows sang. Ravens soared, black against the sun.

When they neared the Carlo's place, Mr. Carlo waved and climbed down the bank toward them. Carlo's full name was Carlo Jachecta, but Natives called him Carlo or Mr. Carlo. Native women who married white men often took their husband's first names as their own last names. Carlo was Italian, a short, powerful man with a barrel chest and thick black hair. He favored red plaid shirts and, like most men in these parts, wore pants with suspenders. His impatience and hot temper sometimes worked against him, but he loved to laugh and cook and was devoted to his family.

Carrying homemade rolls and cranberry preserves, Louise clambered up the rocky embankment with the children. Behind them, Sam and Carlo walked more slowly, talking and laughing.

Mr. Carlo had strung up drying lines and had four smudge fires to smoke the fish and to keep the flies away. Near the fish-wheel were planks set on sawhorses for a table where Julia Carlo cleaned salmon, shee fish, white fish, burbot, and suckers. The fish heads were tossed into buckets of salt water and later made into soup. Fish-head soup had a consistency like cottage cheese and was a great delicacy.

The Carlos lived in a roadhouse built by the Army in the late 1800s and later abandoned. The long, low building had a series of rooms and a central hall, much like a barracks. Sheds at each end once housed sled dogs and horses used by the military.

While Sam, Louise, Julia, and Carlo traded news and gossip, Carlo layered cheese and noodles into a large baking dish. The children—three Harpers and three Carlos, ages four through thirteen—played outside. The two babies snoozed under mosquito tents on a cot.

The dining room held a long table with benches on either side. Louise and Julia pulled up wooden crates to seat the overflow of children. When the lasagna was ready, plates were set out and Carlo took his place in the captain's chair at the head of the table.

"Odd thing happened last week," Carlo said, pausing to take a plate from his wife. "Heard a noise in the root cellar. Sounded like a scraping, real loud."

The Harper fish wheel, similar to this one, brought up hundreds of salmon each season.

"What was it?" Sam asked.

"That's just it," Carlo buttered a roll. "I looked everywhere. Didn't see a thing. It happened a couple of times."

Julia Carlo concentrated on filling the next plate. She knew such talk made her cousin nervous, and she poured Louise a cup of tea.

"Look, I have bubbles in my tea," Louise said, eager to change the subject.

"Money's coming to you, then," Julia said, her voice light and girlish.

Louise blew carefully on the tea to cool it. "Only if I drink it before they break."

When they finished eating, the children began to punch and tickle one another, quietly so they wouldn't get yelled at. When Flora Jane reached around Elsie to tickle her younger brother, her dangling foot touched the floor, and something jabbed her.

"*Abaa!*" she yelped. Looking down, she saw a silvery piece of metal, like a knife blade, sliding slowly along in a crack between the floorboards.

"*Eenaa!*" Flora Jane said, grabbing her mother's arm. "*Eenaa*-look!"

Still sticking through the crack, the blade now moved in the opposite direction. Louise was absorbed in a conversation about a moose that had charged a tree and she waved away her daughter's hand. The other children were staring at the floor. "*Eenaa!*" With a sigh, Louise turned her daughter.

"*Aat sa gee!*" Louise whispered, as her gaze followed the girl's pointing finger. Pushing herself around, Louise leaned forward for a better look. The silvery object slid back and forth, between the planks, and goose bumps prickled her arms.

Carlo and Julia craned their heads and Sam leaned over the table to see what the excitement was about. "Looks like a knife blade," Sam's voice was strained.

"That does it!" Carlo hollered, his face turning red with fury. He scrambled to his feet and headed for the door, his chair crashing to the floor. Sam was right behind him.

Outside, at the cellar door, Carlo tinkered with the rusty latch, then flung it open. Inside, the root cellar was dark and musty. Daylight leaked through cracks in the floorboards over their heads. As his eyes adjusted to the gloom, Sam noted the dirt walls, a few potatoes sprouting on the floor, a sprinkling of rat droppings. There was no sign of a knife or anything like it. Carlo looked around the empty cellar and snorted in exasperation.

When the two men returned to the dining room, shaking their heads, Julia got up to serve dessert—white cake with blueberries. Sam took another look at the floor near Flora Jane. The blade was gone.

While Carlo and Sam argued about the blade and how it could have moved, Louise had her own ideas. This trick felt sly. Something she'd expect from *Nicolina*. But where had it gone? Well, *Nicolina* were known to disappear. The *Dena* knew their spirits were powerful.

Despite the heat, the afternoon had taken on a spooky chill.

Louise loved cake but her appetite was gone. The lasagna was a lump in her stomach and her tea was cold, the bubbles flat.

"We have to get back," she said, getting to her feet. Even Sam seemed willing to leave. "The fish-wheel needs work, a spoke's cracked," he said. Carlo nodded. There was always work to be done at fish camp.

Down at the water's edge, Louise and the children, who had been denied dessert in the rush to leave, climbed into the skiff. Wading up to his knees, Sam pushed them farther into the water, then jumped aboard while the Carlos watched from the shore.

The fresh river air was calming and Louise began to relax. She thought of the cake and blueberries. Too bad she hadn't brought them with her as Julia had suggested.

In the middle of the skiff, Flora Jane, Elsie, and Arthur, trying to make themselves comfortable, had similar thoughts. That shiny thing in the floor was spooky. And their mother's nervousness and their dad and Mr. Carlo getting so mad made it even more scary. But now, from the safety of the boat, it sure didn't seem worth missing cake and blueberries.

10

The Deeyninh

An Indian Settlement at Nenana

The old man leaned over Flora Jane's cot and touched her sweaty forehead with dry fingers. His white hair swung forward and caught on the leather cord of his medicine pouch. He smelled of fish and smoke and his ancient words were low and soothing.

Louise Harper pulled on her parka, her round face tight with worry. When the *Deeyninh* motioned to her, they left the house, the door banging behind them.

Snow was thigh-deep on the hill behind the Harper cabin and they were panting when they reached the top. Twenty minutes later they were back at the cabin, stamping snow off their feet, carrying spruce boughs and willow branches. Clouds of icy air rolled off their clothes as the old man slapped his caribou mittens, spraying bits of ice in a faint pattern of wet spots on the floor. The slamming door and rush of cold air roused the girl.

"*Eenaa*" Flora Jane whimpered. The *Deeyninh* began tying thin willow branches around her wrists. Beyond him, she saw her mother feeding spruce boughs into the black stove.

"The smoke will kill the germs," the *Deeyninh* said as he straightened from the cot. He walked stiffly to the stove and propped open the door to allow more of the scent into the room.

"Leave these on her for three days." He pointed to the thin branches on Flora Jane's wrists. "And give her castor oil and a lot of water. Feed her soup and hardtack, nothing else."

"*Anaa Basee,*" Louise said, gratefully. She handed him a package wrapped in brown paper. It contained homemade rolls and part of a moose haunch.

Within a few days, Flora Jane was running around and singing, "Hasn't antee boteee seen Kelleeee?"

A few weeks later, the Harpers moved across the river to Nenana, where Sam found work for the winter. Nenana had a doctor and a hospital. Unknown to Sam, who believed strongly in white medicine and science, Nenana also had Big William.

A distant cousin to Louise, Big William stood several inches over six feet and was the best known *Deeyninh* to come out of the Koyukon region since his grandfather, Chief Larion. Also known as Red Shirt, Chief Larion was the most powerful medicine man in Athabascan memory.

One afternoon, a few months after the move to Nenana, Flora Jane and her mother put on their warmest clothes and walked the six blocks to St. Mark's Mission. Louise had made moccasins, mukluks, and mittens to trade for used clothing donated by churches in the States. About seventy children from outlying villages lived and went to school at St. Mark's, and there was always a need for footgear and mittens.

Flora Jane's imagination was bursting with what she might find in the clothing bins. "I want a red dress!" she chanted in a singsong voice.

In the gray morning light, snow fell in tiny flakes and muffled the sounds of their mukluks. Louise snorted, her breath a white fog in the brittle air. "*Kah!* You need a warm sweater, not a flimsy dress."

At the mission, a large, wood-framed building, Sister Agnes gave Louise a chit for the clothing. "You do such beautiful work, Mrs. Harper," the Sister said, pausing as her wrinkled fingers traced a beaded dogwood blossom on the moccasins.

Louise ducked her head and murmured awkwardly, "Thank you." Sister Agnes understood *basee,* but Louise liked to practice her English.

The clothing was kept in a musty room at the back of the mission. Once an open porch, the enclosed room had a low ceiling and was dimly lit by kerosene lamps. Stacks of men's, women's, and children's clothes covered several wooden tables. Bins of underwear, shoes, and boots stood to the side. Flora Jane began digging through a pile of children's clothes and spotted a red sleeve. It was attached to a small, raggedy coat. Disappointed, she pushed it aside. In another pile, she glimpsed something the color of cranberries. She tugged at it and a woolly sweater sprang loose. It had a heavy cable stitch and was a bit frayed. But she had never seen such a beautiful color. Hugging it to her chest, she called to her mother, *"Eenaa!"*

Louise looked up from a pile of men's jackets. *"Aa tsa ghii ah"* she sighed as she squinted at the shapeless sweater. Flora Jane pulled it over her head, and Louise looked it over. It was big, but that was okay. And she could replace the missing buttons. At least it was a sweater, not a useless dress. She nodded her permission and Flora Jane raced to a scrap of murky mirror nailed to the door. Even with her hair braided so tight her eyes were yanked into slits, the rich color made her feel pretty.

Louise returned to the stack of men's clothes, shaking her head. Red reminded her of too many bad things. Of hoostitutes and leering white men who called Native women squaws and fooked them and beat them.

Still, red ochre, according to the *Dena*, held the sacred power of creation and death. Her ancestors once used the reddest ochre they could find to paint designs on their *baalgaas* for good hunting and fighting. In ceremonies, small pieces of the ochre were carried in medicine pouches worn around the neck. It brings us closer to the spirits of the earth, the elders said.

When Louise and Flora Jane left the mission, they carried children's clothes, a suit jacket for Sam that Louise could alter, and the red sweater. They had barely stepped into the fading daylight when a neighbor, a woman whose name Flora Jane could never remember, Abigail something, called to them. Her eyes were bright and practically out of the side of her mouth, she began whispering to Louise. The woman was so furtive all Flora Jane could make out was something about "a meeting at the Village Hall."

At last, Abigail said, *"Tla tla,"* and Louise and Flora Jane headed for the hall.

When they pushed open the big door, they saw the wooden benches around the edge of the room were filled and more people were sitting on the floor. The hall smelled of sweat, tobacco, and tanning solution. Trying not to jostle anyone in the hushed atmosphere, they made their way to the back where they found a place on the floor.

Still in her parka, Flora Jane began to sweat as she tried to get comfortable. A tall, heavy-set man blocked her view and she stretched up to see around him. At the front of the room she glimpsed a tall, dignified man in a beaded caribou jacket. He was facing the audience while talking to a woman who stood before him. She was crying. A tense man sat next to her, and clinging to his arm was a younger woman with large eyes. Louise leaned toward her daughter.

"That's Big William in the beaded jacket."

Big William and the tearful woman talked in Koyukon and there were lengthy pauses between his questions and her murmured answers. Flora Jane could hardly hear them. Worse, her long johns were itching, the hall was hot and stuffy, and she was getting sleepy. When an inhalation of breath swept the room, she stretched up to see.

Big William was wrapping a white cloth around a what looked like a bone. His face stern, he turned to the younger woman with the big eyes. His deep voice carried so much authority that Flora Jane wondered if he was a chief. After a moment, still facing the younger woman, he lifted his hands, made a quick twisting motion, and a blood-red stain appeared, soaking the white cloth. *"AGEE!"* Louise exhaled sharply as gasps filled the room.

Then Flora Jane heard a soft hissing rise all around her. It was the sound to ward off evil.

The young woman's hand fell away from the man's arm and she sagged. *"Nideenh!"* she whispered. The man had turned a yellowish green, as if he had eaten something bad.

As people left the hall, they clustered outside, talking among themselves. The sky was dark by the time Flora Jane and her mother left the hall. Without pausing, they started for home.

"What was that man doing?" Flora Jane said, trotting to keep up with her mother. "Was that really blood? Where did it come from?"

Snow was falling in a thick curtain of small, dense flakes, a sign that more snowfall was coming. Big flakes meant a light snowfall, soon over. Louise gave her daughter a quick look.

"Big William is a powerful *Deeyninh,*" she said after a moment. "He was helping that woman with a problem."

"What kind of problem?" The snow was slippery and Flora Jane struggled to stay on her feet. "Who was that man between those women?" Louise didn't answer.

That evening, after the children had gone to bed, Flora Jane tried to stay awake, hoping her mother would tell her father about the *Deeyninh.* Sam was reading *Collier's* magazine at the table when Flora Jane heard her mother say, ". . . Big William questioned the wife."

Sam gave her an impatient look. Ignoring it, Louise continued. "Then he turned to the other woman and said, 'If you keep seeing this woman's husband, you will injure your head. You might die . . .'" Louise was moving around the room and her voice faded.

"Then he twisted the handkerchief." Her voice was suddenly clear. "And blood poured out!" Sam slapped the magazine down on the table and Flora Jane jumped.

"*Kyuh!*" Sam snorted in disgust. "He's a faker, he's using superstition to fool you! I don't want our children around such hocus pocus!" All this talk made Sam nervous, although it had been months since he had seen his old girlfriends.

Flora Jane couldn't make out her mother's reply. As her parent's voices droned on, she fell asleep.

One morning, months later, Flora Jane was ironing. She rested the heavy sadiron on the stove to heat while she opened a bundle of laundry on the table. A bright red and white scarf caught her eye and she spread it on the iron board.

Louise was baking rolls and going on about a silly cousin who'd suggested Flora Jane soon would be old enough to be with a man. Louise fumed. "She's such an ignoramus—even if we are related!"

Flora Jane was looking at the scarf. The red was the shade of the sweater she'd found at the mission. Then she remembered the blood-red handkerchief she had seen that day.

"*Eenaa*," she said, "Remember that meeting at the town hall?" Louise looked up from wiping the stove. "And those women? What happened to that pretty woman and the husband she was trying to steal?"

Startled, Louise forgot her cousin. How had her daughter known about that? She sighed. It was impossible to keep secrets in a one-room cabin filled with children. Louise thought back to that day.

"That woman . . ." she recalled, grinning. "She dropped that man like a hot potato. Found herself a single man in another village. She was quick, that one!"

At age eight, Flora Jane didn't understand all the fuss about having a man. *Who wanted one?* From what she'd seen, women did all the work. She sprinkled water on the scarf as her mother had taught her.

"What was in that cloth?" She looked at her mother. "It looked like a moose bone when Big William twisted it, and it turned red."

Steam hissed as she touched the iron to the scarf, and waited for her mother to answer. She was accustomed to her mother taking time to think before she spoke.

Louise still felt the expectant atmosphere in the hall that day, the people holding their breath. And the heightened suspense when Big William twisted the bone. Wringing blood from a bone. Some *Deeyninh* used a dye. But once in awhile a *Deeyninh* came along with so much power he had no need for tricks, a *Deeyninh* who could heal blindness and straighten bones. The power came from the spirit world and who could explain that? Medicine power lay in the respect and silence surrounding it.

"Some people thought it was blood," Louise said, reaching for a broom. She began sweeping up the spilled flour. "Others thought it was a dye."

Flora Jane frowned at the vague answer, then she remembered the *Deeyninh* who had helped when she was so sick. When it was time to cut off the willow bracelet he'd put on her wrists, she had wanted to do it herself. He was standing there when she accidentally jabbed herself with the knife.

"Ah," he said when he saw the blood. "You'll have a long life."

Flora Jane looked at the blood on her wrist, puzzled. She wanted to ask why, but to question a *Deeyninh* was impolite. Sensing her confusion, he murmured, "Don't always look with your eyes."

Flora Jane reached for a dress and smoothed it over the iron board. The faded blue dress had come from St. Mark's Mission. "It was really blood, wasn't it?" she asked. "Big William twisted blood from that bone."

Louise emptied the dustpan, then stood the broom in the corner behind the door.

Through the window, a thin ray of sun lit the room. It was time to feed the dogs.

11

The Owl and the Ship

RAMPART, 1918

Captain Al Mayo, Grandma Mayo and their children and grandchildren.

In late June, Louise and the children visited Cap Mayo's family in their big, two-story house in Rampart. The weather was balmy and the children—four Harpers and three Mayos—begged to go outside.

"Can we climb the hill, *Eenaa*, can we?" Flora Jane pleaded. She was eight, oldest of the assorted Mayo and Harper offspring. Mrs. Mayo nodded at Louise; it was all right with her. Louise looked through the window at the hill behind the house. It led to other streets in Rampart, now deserted.

"*Oho*," she said, "but don't go far!"

The hill behind the Mayo home was covered with willows, birch, alder, and a few roses, fragrant and thorny. Honeybees flew heavily, and mosquitoes, gnats, and no-see-ums swarmed in thick clouds around the children's heads. As they climbed, their store-bought shoes slipped and they had to grab branches to pull themselves along.

Overhead, robins squawked and scolded. Flora Jane remembered the story of the robin's song. A boy robin's sister marries a kingfisher that eats pike entrails. The boy robin sneers and pokes fun at his brother-in-law for slurping up pike guts. Flora Jane began to sing.

> *Do do selenh*
> My brother-in-law down river (around the bend)
> *Kk'oolk'oyh ts' eege'*
> eats pike guts
> *Teelzoot selnee*
> slurps 'em up he said,
> *Salint, salint, salint*
> My brother-in-law, my brother-in-law, my brother-in-law.

In the hot sun, sweat rolled down the their faces as Flora Jane herded the younger ones ahead. She liked bringing up the rear where she could take time to look at things. So far she had seen a bird's nest hidden in the brush and the tiny face of a mouse or shrew, its unblinking black eyes staring at her. A few feet away, she glimpsed the long, furry body of a weasel scurrying through the brush.

When they reached the top, the children rested on an old boardwalk to catch their breath. The wooden walk was split and rickety, with gaps where the boards had rotted and rusty nails lurked. Avoiding it, the children meandered down the middle of Third Street, now overgrown with devils club, foxtails, and crab grass.

Rampart had once been a bustling town. But after epidemics of flu, whooping cough, and measles and after the gold-seekers left for other strikes, the six upper streets that ran parallel to the river held only abandoned houses and cabins.

Dodging thorny weeds, the children stared at the empty buildings. Windows were broken. Doors hung awry, revealing broken floors in parlors and kitchens. A faded sign with a big red cross was propped in front of a small building with peeling white paint. Flora Jane thought it had been a hospital built by the Episcopal Church.

In the distance, they spotted a small house with a porch supported by two posts. Ground frost had heaved one end of the porch higher than the

Archdeacon Stuck with Walter Harper

other. The other children ran ahead to look through the window while Flora Jane followed. To her left, lace curtains fluttered in an open window. As she was about to look inside, she heard a shout.

On the tilted porch ahead, her brother Art, Ben Mayo, and the other children were tumbling over one other and yelling. Untangling themselves, they got up and raced past Flora Jane in a plume of dust, their expressions panicky. The littlest Mayo was wailing.

"What's wrong?" Flora Jane yelled after them.

Getting no answer, she grabbed the porch rail and pulled herself up the tilted steps. Through the cracked, dirty window, she saw a wooden floor covered with dust. Faded blue-pattern wallpaper peeled from the walls. An arched doorway led to a second room, probably a kitchen. Beyond it she glimpsed a door. It most likely led to a shed. If it was like her family's shed, it had a cutting block for splitting wood for the stove and heater. Her gaze returned to the main room and to a small staircase on the right. There were five steps, a landing, a turn, and more steps. Then she saw it.

A huge spotted owl perched on the banister in the gloomy shadows. Caught in its glare, Flora Jane froze. Hardly breathing, she watched as the owl stretched a leathery leg. Then it leaned forward and ruffled its wings. In the dim light, the feathers shimmered from gray to white.

As she stared, her sweaty hands gripping the window ledge slipped and she fell back onto the cockeyed porch with a thud.

At age 20, Walter Harper led Archdeacon Stuck's climbing party to the top of Mt. McKinley.

Bouncing to her feet, she flew off the porch. Leaping over holes in the broken boardwalk, ignoring the rusty nails, she tore through the foxtails and devils club.

When she caught up with the others, she was sweaty and covered with bloody scratches. Leaning over to catch her breath, she glimpsed tear streaks on the dusty faces of the three youngest children. After a moment, without saying a word, they scrambled down the hill.

Flora Jane's mother and Mrs. Mayo were laughing over some bit of gossip when the children raced into the kitchen.

"*Eenaa*, we saw . . . " Elsie gasped.

"There's an owl!" Ben Mayo pointed up the hill. His black hair stuck out every which way and he was covered with twigs. The two mothers raised their eyebrows and looked at one another.

"Come here." Louise pulled John and Arthur closer. "You're filthy!" She wet a cloth and began wiping John's face and hands. Moving to Arthur, she started in on his ears.

"*Abaa*!" he yelped.

"Flora Jane, bring me the cookies." Mrs. Mayo nodded toward the counter while she wiped Ben's grimy hands. Flora Jane dabbed at her hands with a washrag and went to get the cookies.

Munching their oatmeal cookies, the children told their mothers about the owl. "Must be the Judge's owl," Mrs. Mayo said.

"You went that far!" Flora Jane's mother frowned at her.

Flora Jane sighed and finished her cookie. Why were her mother and Mrs. Mayo ignoring the news about the owl? She licked the crumbs from her fingers and wiped her hands on her bib overalls. She'd never understood grownups.

✧ ✧ ✧

A week later, back in Tanana, Flora Jane and her mother were at the table, mending work clothes.

"That owl," her mother said, as she tore off a length of thread with her teeth and looked at Flora Jane. "The one you saw on Third Street. It belonged to Judge Wright. Some man gave him a young owl he'd found, for some legal work. The judge had it for years. When it died, he had it stuffed, kept it on the stairs."

Flora Jane stared at her, her mouth open. "But its wings . . . I saw it move."

"Hootlani!" Louise hissed nervously. Taking a breath, she picked up a needle and a spool of green thread. "Remember the story about Raven and the Owl? How Raven gave all the birds jobs and saved the worst for Owl. Know why?" Flora Jane shook her head. "Because Owl always looked so wise and Raven could never get the best of him." Louise threaded the needle and reached for a torn work shirt.

Needle flashing, she continued, "Raven told Owl, when you hoot, you'll warn people that someone close to them will die. And if you show yourself in the daytime, many souls will go to the headwaters of the Yukon. That's what Raven told Owl." Louise picked up her sewing scissors. "Stuffed owls don't count!"

✧ ✧ ✧

A few months later, in October, Flora Jane's uncle, Walter Harper, and his bride, Frances Wells, left Alaska. Walter had military duty to fulfill. The couple was going to Philadelphia where Frances would stay with her father while Walter served in the Army.

In 1913, when Walter was twenty, he had led Archdeacon Stuck's climbing party to the top of Mt. McKinley, or Denali as the Natives called it. McKinley, at over 20,320 feet, is the tallest mountain in North America, and Walter became the first climber to reach the top. The climb took three months and Stuck later published *Ascent of Denali* to chronicle their achievement. Early editions contain pages from Walter's journal.

Walter met his bride at the mission hospital in Fort Yukon as he recovered from typhoid fever. Frances had pale blue eyes, brown hair, and a smile that could charge a room.

In Fort Yukon, where they were married a few weeks earlier by Archdeacon Stuck, they caught a boat to Whitehorse. From there, they took the narrow-gauge railway to Skagway, where they were to board the *Princess Sophia* bound for Seattle. The 111-mile rail trip wound through the White Pass and took most of the day. They arrived in Skagway at 5:30 that evening.

Nestled at the foot of steep, snow-topped mountains, Skagway was bursting with travelers hoping to catch the last boat out before winter. A dusting of fresh snow was creeping down the mountainside, and the air had the feel of winter approaching.

Finally, at seven o'clock Captain Locke of the S.S. *Princess Sophia* ordered the gangway lowered for boarding. Walter and Frances made their way through the crowds to their cabin. Excited about their first trip together, they explored the decks and lounge. Built in Scotland, the *Princess Sophia* was a four-year-old passenger and freight steamer. She was licensed to carry a maximum of 500 passengers and a crew of seventy. At ten o'clock, after much preparation, the *Princess Sophia* sounded her whistle and pulled away into the night.

Heading south, the *Sophia* would steam through the Lynn Canal to Juneau. Around midnight, when most passengers were in bed or in the salon playing cards, the *Sophia* suddenly found herself in the midst of a ferocious gale.

About this time, the first mate discovered they had strayed a mile off course.

Midway between Skagway and Juneau, Vanderbilt reef loomed beneath the water. At low tide, it was just a just a few feet below the surface, covering half an acre near the center of the canal where the shipping lane narrowed to two and a half miles. The reef was the flat top of a mountain, marked by a small red and black buoy. The buoy was easy to see in daylight. At night it was invisible.

By early the next morning, the *Sophia* battled heavy rollers and whitecaps. A strong north wind whistled over the mountains bringing with it heavy snow. In the blinding storm, the *Sophia*, cruising eleven to twelve knots, ran aground the submerged mountain top with a crunch that vibrated the 2,320-ton ship to her core. Her bow lifted out of the water as she slid to a stop with a grinding jolt, flinging her crew about and knocking passengers from their beds.

The *Sophia*'s hull, partly afloat in the low tide, scraped the rocks and her engine screws rotated uselessly. A shaken Captain Locke ordered the engines turned off. In the silence, the howling wind and creaks and groans of the ship

Walter Harper and his bride, Frances Wells, died in the sinking of the S.S. Sophia.

further alarmed the frightened passengers. The storm was too fierce to launch the lifeboats. The *Sophia's* wireless operator radioed for help, "If you don't come soon, it will be too late."

Over the next several hours, ten ships responded to the call, but none could reach the *Sophia* for fear of crashing into her or grounding themselves. As the ship's hull shifted and grated against the reef, the passengers prayed, slept, wrote letters, and comforted children.

The next morning, the storm worsened, forcing the other ships to find windbreaks behind islands and in coves. When high tide returned, heavy winds and waves swung the *Sophia* into a 180-degree turn. As she twisted and slid into the rising tide, the rocky reef tore out her hull and water gushed into the engine and boiler rooms. Heavy bunker oil spilled out and congealed in the freezing water.

Icy water rushed in through shattered portholes and boilers exploded. Passengers and crew ran for the lifeboats and began leaping from the deck. The wind-blown spray was heavy with bunker oil and weighed down their clothing. All ten lifeboats capsized.

The next day, in the high tide and under some clearing in the sky, all that could be seen of the *Princess Sophia* was her mast.

Over the next several weeks, volunteers in Juneau worked in twenty-four hour shifts, cleaning the bodies and determining identities.

Walter and his bride were buried in Juneau.

Flora Jane and her family escaped the
Spanish flu by moving to Nenana.

12

The Big Flu

Building the Alaska Railroad.

In the fall of 1917, a young beluga whale was seen swimming from the Bering Sea into the lower Yukon. "It probably took a wrong turn at St. Michael's," people joked, unnerved by the unusual event.

The following spring, two Athabascan hunters stopped off in North Nenana at the Harpers' cabin. Frost had whitened their eyebrows and the wolverine ruffs of their parkas.

"*Abaa aahaa kk' ohoodoyh*," one said, his voice low as they discussed the sickness with Sam and Louise. "People are dying in so many villages." It was April 1918. The Spanish flu had reached Alaska.

After the hunters left, Sam looked at Louise. "There's no doctor here, no medicine, we have to get to Nenana." What locals called North Nenana was a construction camp for the Alaska Railroad. The camp had a cookhouse and tin shed. Several Native families lived nearby.

The town of Nenana was two miles south and across the Tanana River. Including the surrounding area, it had a population of about 2,000, most of

73

whom were white. Nenana also had a doctor, hospital, school, mission, and several saloons. A bridge was to be built at Nenana for the new railroad, but in the meantime the river was best crossed in a boat, or over hard-frozen ice in winter. Spring was a risky time to make a crossing.

Sam had a nervous feeling in his gut as he pulled on his parka and mukluks and went out to get the sled and dogs ready. With breakup nearing, this was their last chance to cross the river while it was still frozen. If they waited to cross by boat, they might all have the flu.

Louise and Flora Jane packed cooking utensils, bedding, tools, and the beadwork needles Louise had traded for in Tanana. As she worked, Louise remembered the whale. The *Dena* knew when something unusual occurred in nature, something—usually bad—happened to the people. She remembered a dream of her father's.

"The world exploded, there was fire and guns and men dying all around, and lights going off in the sky," he'd told her, looking shaken. A few months later, war broke out in Europe.

The Harper's four dogs were tied to stumps. When Sam dragged out the nine-foot sled, they whined, yelped, and danced on their toes. Working quickly, Sam unfolded a canvas tarp inside the sled, then unrolled a moose hide on top, fur side up. The moosehide would keep the children dry and the sled buoyant if they went through the ice.

Inside the cabin, Louise and Flora Jane hurriedly dressed Elsie, Arthur, and the baby, John. They wore long johns, bib overalls, cloth parkas, mukluks, and mittens. Louise, eight months pregnant, wore her clothes in layers— three skirts, one over the other and, under her cloth parka, a long-sleeved blouse, a plaid-flannel shirt, and two sweaters. Sam and the children also dressed in layers. It was the best way to carry their clothes since the sled was so crowded.

After harnessing the dogs, Sam returned to the cabin, his breath making white clouds in the air, even though it was nearly May. "Ready?" he asked, picking up the food box. Louise nodded as she pulled the *gits*, mittens on a string, through the sleeves of the baby's parka. "Let's go," Sam said, pushing the door open with his shoulder as he carried the food box to the sled.

Outside in the crisp air, Flora Jane climbed into the sled, followed by Elsie, Arthur, and the baby, all sitting spoon fashion. Sam rechecked the dog harnesses while Louise wrapped the moosehide around the children, then tied them, crisscross, into the sled with rope. The dogs yelped and whined, eager to run.

Last, Sam tied Louise to the handlebars, allowing a few feet of rope to dangle between her and the sled. If she fell, the rope was her security. At the head of the team, Sam lashed himself to the lead dog, Queenie, and picked up his pole. "*Hieee!*" he yelled, and the excited dogs took off. Nenana was two miles away.

The runners made a whishing sound over the snow as the dogs settled into a steady run. Louise took a deep breath and tried not to worry about the river. On either side of the narrow trail, branches bore hard little buds that soon would burst into pussy willows. Overhead, bare limbs glistened with crystallized snow. Louise remembered elders saying, "When wind blows, but the snow on the branches doesn't fall, sickness will come."

The sled swayed over the ice-encrusted snow with a crackling sound. Then, abruptly, they reached the river, and Sam brought the team to a halt. The Tanana was half a mile wide and still hard, but lakes of river-melt were forming over the crust. Sam's ulcer burned with worry. He couldn't lead the huskies straight across to Nenana, too much soft ice in the way. He'd have to zigzag across, testing the ice with a pole as he went, working around the soft ice. This would take twice as long to reach Nenana, but they had no choice.

Before he lost his courage, Sam yelled, "*Hieee!*" and the team started out on the ice, moving cautiously. Securely lashed to Queenie, Sam prodded the ice ahead and on either side, testing its strength.

A whistling, cold wind made the children even more jittery. Behind them, Louise shouted, "See that dock? That's Nenana, don't let it out of your sight!"

For the next hour, the children locked their eyes on the dock, spinning their heads like owls as the sled went one direction, then the other. At times Sam found himself knee-high in the freezing water atop the frozen crust of the river, and the team had to dog paddle.

With the ice creaking and shifting under their weight, the nervous dogs whined and scrambled to keep their balance. Twice, Prince and King, two of the heavier dogs, broke through but managed to scrabble out, their toenails digging into the soft ice.

The frightened children could feel the river pulsating beneath the sled, and they stared longingly at the dock. Behind the sled, Louise slipped and fell so often, she lost count. On the shore, townspeople had gathered. "Go this way, the ice is harder . . . now go that way!" they yelled, waving their arms. Their encouraging voices cut through the wind and even the dogs seemed to grow more confident and sure-footed.

About twenty feet from the dock, Sam and Queenie reached a strip of roaring black water. Without pausing, they leaped into the churning river. The dogs' whining grew louder as they followed. Behind them, the sled bobbed in the rapid current. Louise let go of the handlebars knowing her weight would drag the sled under and felt the rope around her stomach tighten. Her soaked clothes dragged her under. Choking and coughing, her hands and feet quickly numbing, she managed to keep her head above water.

Meanwhile, at the Nenana dock, two men climbed into a small boat and were rowing out to meet them. Sam lifted his pole and one of the men grabbed the other end.

People screamed from the dock, "You're gonna make it! Come on, you're gonna make it!" The children and Sam heard them but all Louise heard was the roar of the ice-choked river.

Then, in a flurry of activity, Sam, the dogs, and the sled were pulled onto the dock. When Louise emerged, round as a kewpie doll, the townspeople were shocked. "You're pregnant!" a man blurted. His wife pushed by him and began untying Louise and the children from the sled. Protected by the moose hide, the children weren't even damp.

"Are you hurt?" the woman asked. Louise could barely stand and her lips were blue. "Just wet," she said, then her legs gave out and she collapsed.

At first the Harpers were parceled out to several Native families. Then Sam rented a one-room cabin, about ten by fourteen feet with a wood stove. It also had a swayback double bed, a cot, tall dresser, armoire with a large drawer, and a table with three wooden crates for chairs. Behind the cabin was an outhouse. A community well was not far away.

Flora Jane and Elsie shared the cot. Art and John slept in the open drawer of the armoire. Soon the family had canned goods on the shelves and a cord of wood stacked outside.

One evening, Sam didn't come home from work. When he failed to appear by the next morning, Louise, who now had the flu, grew frantic. All the children were sick and she was soon due to give birth. She dropped her head back on the flattened pillow, damp with sweat.

"Flora Jane," she said, irritably. "Fix us something to eat . . . and go to the well, we need water." Flora Jane wanted to cry she was so weary. Lightheaded and dizzy, she pulled on her parka and mukluks. The sloped ground around the well was icy and the girl duck-walked as she approached it. When she stretched over well wall to lower the bucket, her feet lifted off the ground.

"Be careful!" someone said. The concern in the man's voice was the first kindness she had heard in weeks and she started to bawl. Startled, he grabbed her baggy overalls and pulled her back from the well. Flora Jane was crying so hard that she could hardly see him.

Louise had been dreaming of a whale in a river and dead people on the shore when she awoke and saw a white man with a brown beard bending over her. In delirium, she saw him look around the cold, dark room, then proceed to build a fire in the stove.

His name was Francis, he told her later as he emptied the trash and swept the floor. He was a shipbuilder, working as a carpenter on the new town hall. "I had a wife and child but they died—smallpox." He began washing the children's feverish faces and sweaty hands. "My daughter was about her age," he said, looking at Flora Jane, now burning with fever on the cot.

Francis changed their bedding and put clean underwear on John and Art. A pile of smelly linen grew in the corner by the door. Before taking it to a laundry, he heated chicken soup, and served it with canned pears and toast. Three times a day for a week, Francis came and fixed the same meal. Toast, pears, and soup. Morning, noon, and night.

At first, Louise and the children were too sick to eat more than a bite of toast and a spoonful of soup. Later, when their appetites returned, they were sick of the menu. But they were clean and nourished and the house was aired and warm.

Days later, Francis learned everyone in North Nenana, more than a hundred people, had died of the flu. He also found Sam, who had collapsed on the street and was in the hospital where he was recuperating.

Francis found a midwife for Louise. When she gave birth to a boy, Louise said, "I want to name him after you." She looked up at the tall man to see if this was all right. Francis looked at the dark-skinned baby, then at Louise. Gripping her hand, he smiled.

Entering a White World

✧ ✧ ✧

Leaving village and bush life for Fairbanks and a cash economy took a heavy toll on the Harpers. As the family grew so did its poverty, increasing the stress between Sam and Louise. It seemed that every time he looked at her she got pregnant.

My mother's eyes sparkled when she described Grandma's feisty nature in handling adversity. About her own years at the University of Alaska she was less buoyant.

"I don't like to think about that," she said, "it was too hard, I had to work all the time."

She had been exhausted, frequently ill, and she'd had few friends at the university. Yet, when she saw former white classmates on the street or at the Loussac library where she worked, she smiled and talked. She had mentioned her aunts so often, I could almost hear their voices. "Smile, Flora Jane, smile. People will like you if you smile."

*Sam's sister, Marianne, helped Sam arrange to send
his children to a boarding school in Oregon.*

13

The Chemawa Years

Louise, baby Walt and Francis

Following the Big Flu, the Harpers stayed in Nenana where Sam worked as a janitor for the Alaska Railroad. He and Louise now had five children with another on the way, forcing Sam to build a second room onto their one-room cabin. With so many mouths to feed, he and Louise were growing desperate. His railroad salary might be sufficient for two adults and two children, but hardly for seven and counting.

"I don't know how I'm going to do it," he complained one afternoon to his sister, Marianne, at the Nenana school where she taught.

Marianne Harper Mozee and Sam's other sister, Margaret, had acquired in California what relatives called "piss elegant" style. Today, she wore a navy print dress with a white lace collar and navy-and-white spectator pumps. Her hair was cut stylishly in a bob. Powder and a touch of color highlighted her cheekbones and generous mouth. The sight of her was enough to stop Native children dead in their tracks.

"Our house is too small," Sam complained. "Even with the room I built on. And children eat so much!" Sam leaned against a long, scarred, wooden table staring out the window. "And Louisie's pregnant again," he said, shaking his head.

Marianne knew her brother had been too proud to accept free housing when the railroad offered it to the Natives. Now the roomy old houses were fully occupied. Sam's decision may have been unfortunate for his family, but she could understand why he wanted to distance himself from the Natives living in the railroad houses.

Half-breeds, bucks, breeders, and Creoles were just a few of the names Sam and his brothers were called. Full-blooded Natives and whites considered the Harper sons and others like them misfits. Attractive half-breed women such as Marianne and Margaret, however, were sought out by white men of position and property.   Sam got to his feet. "I'm thinking about sending the four oldest to an orphanage I heard about in Kansas. It's either that or starve."

Marianne's husband, Ben Mozee, was superintendent of schools. That evening, after Marianne told him of Sam's dilemma, Ben hiked over to the Harper's house. Finding Sam outside chopping wood, Ben wasted no time getting to the point.

"There's a boarding school in Chemawa, Oregon," he said, a little short of breath. His hair was sticking out, but even so, Ben, a slender, fine-boned man in his early fifties, presented an elegant appearance in his wool three-piece suit, white shirt, and leather shoes. "It's run by the Catholic Church for American Indians. Far as I know, all you'd pay is transportation, plus money for clothing, school events—that sort of thing."

After Ben left, driven away by mosquitoes, Sam for once felt optimism. Now he just had to scrape together the money. Much as he wanted to talk it over with someone, he said nothing to Louise. Ever since he'd mentioned the orphanage in Kansas, Louise cried and carried on at any mention of sending the children away.

Athabascan families with too many mouths to feed sometimes adopted

Louise and two sons, John (left), and Arthur

children to childless couples, or to a family that wanted more children. For Athabascans, this was an act of generosity. But Sam had been raised in a white tradition. Seeing his children in the care of other families would be an unbearable reminder of his failure as a provider.

The next morning Sam was walking through the red-light district on his way to work when he heard, "Mornin', Sam!" He looked over a fence and saw the yellow-haired Sarah on the front steps of her house, shaking a mop. "How're you doin'?"

Her manner, despite the early hour, was bright and cheerful. Sarah was thirty-five, voluptuous, and nearly as tall as Sam. Her hair was a shade of blond that sometimes looked green. Wearing a flimsy, red-flowered wrapper

Elsie (third from left) with friends at Chemawa

tied at the waist, she walked down the steps toward him, her furry mules slapping her heels. Six women lived on the strip and Sam and his brothers knew most of them.

Sam was early for work so he sauntered over to Sarah's white picket fence. It stopped at the edge of the house without wrapping around the property. A fence for looks, a floozy fence, Louise called it, knowing who lived behind it. Leaning against the gate, Sam soon found himself telling Sarah about the school in Oregon and how he wanted to send his four oldest to it in the fall if he could get them there. As he talked, he spit out a bit of tobacco stuck to his tongue. He rolled his own cigarettes and they were always coming apart.

"I've got some money saved," he said, "but I don't know how I'll get the rest . . ." Pushing away from the fence, he frowned. His face was lined, and he looked older than he had only a few weeks ago. As Sam trudged off to work, Sarah pursed her thick lips and stared after him.

◇ ◇ ◇

When the four oldest Harper children left for Chemawa, Oregon, accompanied by their uncle, Ben Mozee, Flora Jane was ten, Elsie eight, Arthur six, and John four. They took the train to Seward, traveling through Anchorage. In Seward, they boarded the Alaska Steamship passenger boat for the five-day trip to Seattle. Riding the train and seeing Anchorage were such adventures they almost forgot to eat. Aboard ship, the children were shocked into silence by the staterooms with indoor toilets, the dining room awash with white linen, glittering glasses and silverware, and a vast array of food.

Louise had sewn cash into Flora Jane's garter belt with strict instructions not to lose it. So it was a relief when they reached Chemawa and Flora Jane handed the money over to the school secretary to put in the bank for her. Arriving in the summer when only five hundred students were on campus helped the Harper children to adjust. Before the trip to Oregon, they had never seen more than twenty people in one place at a time. That fall, the campus grew to 2,000 students.

At four, John Harper was the youngest child attending the Catholic boarding school and one of the most homesick. Missing his mother was bad enough but, being one of the smallest and youngest boys, he was also a target for bullies.

Flora Jane arranged with a dining room matron for the Harpers to sit together during meals. The school encouraged children to mingle and to make new friends, but John was so young and they were so far from home, the matron obliged. One afternoon, the main course at lunch was meatballs. There were eight meatballs on the platter and eight children at the table. Next to John at the end of the table sat a large nine-year-old boy. When the platter reached him, the boy scooped out the last two meatballs. Flora Jane, who was watching, jumped to her feet.

"You took my brother's meatball!" she yelled. When the boy reached for his spoon, Flora Jane grabbed the heavy platter and smashed it on his head. Gravy and bits of broken crockery flew across the table and onto floor. The matron came running.

"What's going on, what happened?" she demanded. Flora Jane stood over the boy, who was holding his head and moaning. "This bully stole my brother's meatball," she said, her eyes snapping with anger.

To keep everyone organized, Chemawa students marched wherever they went, even to meals. They were drilled so often, their "squad right" and "squad left" were perfect. For Sunday review, they wore uniforms. After two years, Flora Jane was thrilled when she was made drill captain in charge of the little girls' team. On Sundays, about fifty little girls, ages six to eight, were so excited it was agony to wait while the older students' teams performed. Flora Jane had drilled them every afternoon until they found themselves marching in their dreams. They lived for Sundays.

"Companeeeee march!" Flora Jane bellowed, her voice much bigger than her slight 5-foot-3 figure. "Left, right! Left, right!"

The sky overhead was a bright blue and everyone was warm. All the little girls wore navy jackets with pleated skirts, white blouses and bobby socks and shiny, black leather shoes. As company leader, Flora Jane also wore a navy cape lined with scarlet. One side was carefully turned back over her shoulder to reveal the vivid lining.

"Left oblique!" she called out, and the little girls marched crisply in formation, fanning out flawlessly. When Flora Jane yelled, "Right oblique!" like a kaleidoscope, the girls twirled into right diagonal lines, their skirts flipping smartly. Cheers, whistling, and clapping erupted from the viewing stands.

Marching backward, facing the girls, Flora Jane twirled her white baton high over her head. "Companeeeee HALT!" The little girls stamped to a halt, the fine dust rising on the parade grounds, and the crowd roared its approval.

✧ ✧ ✧

There was no money from home so visiting Alaska was out of the question. In the summers Flora Jane, Elsie, Arthur, and John, when he was older, earned sixty to eighty dollars each, picking berries and working in a nearby cannery. The first thing they bought were season tickets to basketball and football games and other sporting events. Most students had jobs except for those rich Oklahoma Indians. They had nice clothes, some even had cars. The Harpers wasted no time finding work. Besides their summer jobs for the farmers around Chemawa, they helped out during the school year in the cafeteria.

Aunt Margaret

The summer Flora Jane reached tenth grade she lived with and worked for a doctor and his family in Portland who paid her $25 a month. Like Flora Jane, Elsie also worked for a Portland family and both girls decided to attend Grant High School in Portland. Possessing few personal clothes, they made do, giving their Chemawa uniforms some variety with jewelry and scarves. But the cheap jewelry fell apart, their scarves faded in the wash, and the cute shoes hurt their feet.

When Flora Jane learned her credits were insufficient to graduate with the other seniors at Grant High, she returned to Chemawa with Elsie.

Then Flora Jane came down with tuberculosis and was in the hospital nearly a year. To fatten her up, the nurses and doctors fed her milkshakes and other creamy desserts she grew to hate. Filled with nervous energy, she began sneaking out in the afternoons to play tennis. One afternoon her doctors, watching from the stands, squinted in disbelief when they saw their patient racing around the court during a tournament.

In 1929, their lives changed unexpectedly. Chemawa and other boarding schools across the nation closed for lack of funding during the Depression. Thousands of students were sent home.

Back in Alaska after a decade's absence, the four Harpers were shocked to find six younger brothers and sisters living with their parents in a small house

Aunt Marianne

in Fairbanks. Although Sam had written announcing each new child, it hadn't sunk in that an entire second family had replaced them.

The house grew miserably crowded. Flora Jane and Elsie argued constantly and refused to share a bedroom. Instead Flora Jane claimed the sofa in the living room, while Elsie took over a tiny bedroom in the lean-to Sam had added onto the house. Connie, ten, found herself sharing a cot with eight-year-old Weese. Connie was so young when the four oldest left in 1920 she had little memory of them.

"Why are these big people staying with us?" Connie asked her mother. These strangers weren't like other visitors who stayed a few days, then went home, usually down-river someplace.

"They're home now," Louise said, not looking too happy herself. The cramped quarters were getting on everyone's nerves.

Years of painful homesickness had left the four older Harpers deeply resentful. Sometimes they wondered why their father hadn't sent them to the Nenana Mission School.

In Fairbanks, however, Flora Jane saw young Natives her age who were already "regular drinkers" and showing signs of bad teeth, poor nutrition, and tuberculosis. "Dad was probably right in sending us to Chemawa," she told John.

Remembering his early Chemawa years, John had his doubts. "If we'd stayed here," Flora Jane said, thoughtfully, "we might not even be alive."

Years later they learned—much to their amusement—that their stateside education had been helped along by the hoostitutes of Nenana.

14

Connie

Second Avenue in Fairbanks

Scrunched in a dark corner of the kitchen, on the faded linoleum behind the washing machine, Connie rested her forehead against her bony knees. She was shaking with rage. All the quarters, nickels, dimes, pennies, and half-dollars she'd earned babysitting and kept in a Mason jar in the basement had disappeared. The money she was saving to go to Haskell Institute so she could be a secretary. It was all gone.

Leaning her head against the wall, she realized nothing was hers anymore. Elsie had taken her bed and Connie had to sleep with Weese. All Connie's clothes came from her older sisters, and pretty sorry most of them were, too.

Connie was christened Helen after Helen Callahan, but there were four other Helens in her class at school. When the frazzled teacher asked what she wanted to be called, she thought fast. "Constance," she said. "Constance Harper." Well, at least she'd gotten to choose her name.

Connie thought she knew who had taken her money. The week before, her older brother John had been poking around in the basement. The whole house heard him whoop when he found the pearl-handled gun in their mother's old sewing belt. Louise had barreled down those rickety stairs and snatched the pistol out of John's big hands quicker than you could say Jack Robinson!

A few weeks later, walking home after the first day of school, Connie saw Tim. At twelve, the big white kid scared her. Before she could duck her head and scurry away, he spotted her.

"Hey, Siwash, you stinking Indian!" the boy yelled gleefully. Then Tim and his buddy Ralph laughed as if she was the ugliest thing in the world. Gripping her books to her bony chest, Connie walked faster. When a rock hit her arm, she ran.

The next afternoon, Connie had gone a block or so when she heard a shout and felt a sharp blow behind her ear. Then a second rock hit her shoulder and she spilled her books. The next thing she knew, she was flat on her face on the boardwalk. "You're nothing but a Siwash!" Tim screamed.

Tim kicked her. "Stinking, dirty Indian, why don't you go back to the woods to your teepee!" Spittle flew from his mouth. Connie tasted blood and dust.

"Someone's coming, come on!" Ralph said, grabbing Tim's arm. Half a block away, two white-haired ladies approached. With a final kick to Connie's stomach, his boot scraping her knuckles bloody, Tim jumped off the sidewalk and the boys took off.

After a moment, Connie got to her hands and knees. Spots danced in front of her eyes as she caught her breath. Slivers and bits of rock were embedded in her hands and arms and she saw a long gash on her knee. Probing her mouth with her tongue, she flinched at a loose tooth. Grabbing the railing, she pulled herself to her feet, unaware she was crying.

"Oh my . . . oh dear," the women said. Their voices sounded miles away. "Are you alright, dear?" one asked, frowning at Connie's bruised and bloodied face. Connie's eyes were streaming and she had hiccups. She nodded and wiped her nose with her sleeve, not caring about manners.

"That looked like Ralph Thomas and Tim Shields. Scoundrels, both of 'em," the second woman said as she picked up Connie's books.

When Connie got home, John was in the kitchen eating a peanut butter and jelly sandwich. His smirk faded when he saw her. "What happened to you?"

John Harper

Connie dumped her books on the table. Still feeling wobbly, she went to the sink, wet a towel, and dabbed at her face. She felt a buzzing numbness in one eye. John stared at her. She was going to have some shiner.

"That bully, Tim!" Connie said, trying not to cry again. "He threw rocks and he beat me up. He called me a Siwash!" Fresh tears streamed down her face and she leaned on the sink to catch her breath.

"Tim? Who's Tim?" John, at fourteen, was not much bigger than Tim. But after ten years at Chemawa, John was an aggressive fighter.

"Who's Tim?" he said again. "What's he look like?" Between hiccups, Connie told him.

When Louise got home from cleaning the Bennett's house, she took a look at the cut behind Connie's ear. The girl's thick black hair had crusted with dried blood. Louise got out her scissors and cut away the hair, then poured Listerine mouthwash into the wound. Louise figured that was better than whiskey. The next day, Connie tried to cover the bald spot with her hair, tilting her head to one side to keep it in place.

"Got a crick in your neck?" John asked, grinning. Connie glared at him, but her swollen face wouldn't cooperate. For the next week, he sauntered along when Connie went to school and he was there to meet her when school was over. Connie's friend Liza was impressed. Both girls were a little intimidated by Connie's big brother and said little as they walked home, on the lookout for Tim Shields.

A few days later, John was nowhere to be seen when the girls got out of school. They were a few blocks from Liza's house when Tim and Ralph suddenly appeared on the other side of the railroad tracks. "Hey Siwash!" Tim hollered, bounding toward Connie.

Liza let out a yelp and started running, but Connie froze. As Tim raced hell-bent toward her, she heard another, deeper voice. "Hey you! Stupid!" Turning, she saw her brother walk out from behind an old building.

"Gotta pick on the girls, huh?" John headed straight for Tim, who slowed down when he saw the big Native kid. When John danced a few steps forward, Tim tried to get his feet to move in reverse. Connie still hadn't moved. Her mouth open, she watched bug-eyed as her brother beat the bejesus out of Tim.

❖ ❖ ❖

"Where'd he come from?" Tim muttered to Ralph a few days later. "Where'd she get a brother all of a sudden?"

As word spread about the older brother who stood up to Tim Shields, classmates who had ignored Connie now started talking to her. For the skinny Native girl in raggedy-ass clothes, it was a quite a change. Maybe having John around wasn't so bad after all.

15

Ladies of the Line

FAIRBANKS, 1926

Houses of Prostitution, Fairbanks

One winter afternoon while Louise was away cleaning houses, five-year-old Weese reached up and pulled the handle of a frying pan on the stove. Hot grease flew over her bare arms and face and the little girl screamed.

Connie, seven, was folding laundry in the other room, and she ran into the kitchen. When she saw the spilled grease and pan on the floor, she pulled Weese out the door, not bothering with parkas, and began running, half dragging the little girl toward town to find a doctor.

They had gone a block or so when Connie saw a tall, well-dressed white woman in front of a white-painted house. "What happened? What's wrong, did she hurt herself?"

The woman was powdered and rouged and smelled like flowers. Lines crinkled between her eyes as she looked at Weese's splotchy face. Connie was almost as hysterical as Weese and neither girl could catch her breath to talk.

"Bring her inside," the woman said. "I know about burns. Hurry, bring her over here!"

Connie tugged Weese up the steps into the woman's kitchen. Pulling off

93

her wrap, the woman quickly wet towels in ice water and wrapped them around Weese's arm, neck, and face. Then she put a salve on the burn. Both girls were sniffling, but soon quieted when the woman made tea and gave them each a cookie.

That afternoon, Connie silenced her sister with a glare when their mother Louise came home and saw Weese's bandaged arm and burned face.

"She pulled the pan off the stove and burned herself. I put ice on it and bandaged it," Connie told her mother, having practiced the explanation. Louise looked at the neat bandage, then at her two daughters. She decided there were some things she didn't have to know.

Connie never knew the woman's name, but whenever the woman saw the two girls, she invited them inside for cookies. In private, Connie told Weese, "You want more cookies from that woman? Then don't tell Mom, you hear?"

Young as she was, Connie knew how her mother felt about women in the red light district.

✦ ✦ ✦

When Donny—the baby of the Harper tribe—was six, Lulu Crippin, a Negro prostitute known as "A Lady of Fourth Avenue," owned a house across the street.

Every Sunday Lulu invited Don or Mary over for fried chicken. She never invited more than one at a time because she wasn't used to having kids around. But she always sent them home with a bag of chicken.

Don and Mary were fascinated by Lulu's white Victorian house, its flush toilets, brocaded furniture, and the shiny floor in the kitchen "so clean you could eat off it."

16

Ice Fog

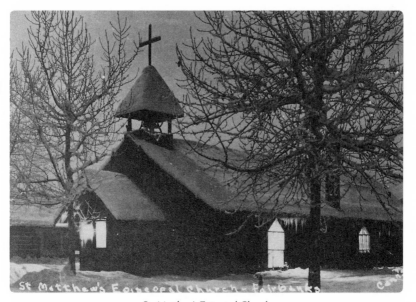

St. Matthew's Episcopal Church

A few weeks before Thanksgiving, the air in Fairbanks crackled with a sudden temperature drop to 40 below zero. Millions of tiny ice crystals hung suspended in the air. They filtered the landscape, softening the deep red of the Nevada Bar to a pale rose. In the foggy distance the old schoolhouse gained in stature, as smaller buildings around it disappeared in the thickened air. And city hall, so ordinary in the sunshine, now seemed mammoth, looming through the gauzy landscape.

Inside her log house on Fifth Avenue, Louise pulled the curtain halfway across the window. Seeing the ice fog made her feel hazy. She wondered if she was ill, some strange ailment, maybe?

Rousing herself, she pulled on a thick brown sweater and began rinsing carrots and celery for supper. She had already brought the meat inside.

The log cache built on stilts protected their food from roving dogs and the occasional bear or wolf that strayed into town.

A few weeks before, a moose had rammed the cache, cracking one of the stilts. Such odd behavior. Surely the moose wasn't interested in the fish or meat? Louise chewed her lip. Unusual events in nature meant trouble.

Cooking odors and the animal smells of furs, hides, wet parkas, and mukluks filled the cabin. Beneath the smoke from a coal-burning stove wafted the tangy aroma of baby urine. Louise used it to tan hides.

"It softens the skins like nothing else," she told her daughters. The girls weren't impressed. As soon as they had jobs, they bought boots and shoes at Northern Commercial. How would they get boyfriends with baby urine wafting up from their feet?

Seven of the Harper children slept on cots and the couch in the two bedrooms and main room. The two babies slept in the cluttered bedroom with Louise and Sam. Flora Jane had moved on campus at the University of Alaska, but often came home at night to help with the babies.

Louise pushed a strand of black hair into her bun and frowned as she looked around for her glasses. Her dark eyes were red-rimmed with fatigue. Glancing at the calendar Sam had brought home from the railroad, she was surprised to see it was almost Thanksgiving. Could they afford a turkey? Usually the Harpers, like other Native families, ate moose, caribou, beaver, or fish. Louise sighed. Her family would certainly welcome a change from moose and fish, briny and salty even after several rinsings.

She took potatoes from a bin and began peeling them with a small knife. From where she stood, even with the curtain pulled halfway across the window, she could see the flatbed of Sam's truck. It had been weeks since the accident with the jack. How much would it cost to get that truck fixed?

She unwrapped the moose meat and spread it out on a cutting board. The meat was tough, having come from a four-year-old. Using her sharpest knife, she cut it into small cubes. Sam was so good about taking care of the truck, but she hadn't seen him work on it lately. Must be something he couldn't handle. Well, Donny was safe, anyway. Her baby had been right there when the jack collapsed.

Louise's memory of the event was vague. Just thinking about it wore her out. *Hootlani!* When the cast-iron skillet was half filled with searing meat, Louise added the carrots, diced potatoes, celery, and onions. Soon the aroma of moose stew filled the house.

The front door opened and Flora Jane came in with a blast of cold air.

"Hi, Mom," she said. Freezing weather had heaved the threshold and Flora Jane gave the door a hard shove to shut and latch it.

"*Do' eenta' aa*," Louise said as she sprinkled celery salt on the stew. Anything to improve the taste. She'd already added garlic and bay leaves.

"Dinner's almost ready." Louise opened the breadbox and pulled out the loaf Sally Mayo had left on the table. Why were people bringing food? Yesterday her friend Lillian had come by with a warm cheese and noodle casserole. Just up from a nap, Louise had been too drowsy to ask why. People brought food when there was a celebration or illness or some catastrophe. But why the Harpers?

Howls interrupted her confused thoughts. Mary and Donny were awake. Flora Jane pulled off her coat and headed toward the bedroom. Louise turned back to the stew, stirring, adding water, and tasting.

Outside it was colder. Fifty below tonight maybe. Usually Louise did not think in terms of temperatures. It was cold or it was colder. Like all Natives, Louise knew what you could do in certain weather and what you couldn't. Like bury somebody.

Kyuh! Now why would she think that? Well, as if it mattered, she learned since moving to Fairbanks that a winter burial is possible. Extra graves were dug in the fall before the ground froze hard as a rock. If too many people died, the bodies were stored in the mortuary until spring thaw. Louise stopped. What was she thinking? Burials instead of ice fog! *Hootlani!*

A second burbling yell erupted from her youngest daughter. Flora Jane was rinsing out a washcloth and Maribeth, recognizing the signs of a bath, had started jabbering.

"I want to bathe Mary and Donny first, Mom," Flora Jane called out. "I'll eat later." Washrag baths, or spit baths, were more common than tub baths in the winter when water was scarce and the cold, dry air made your skin itchy.

"*Ts'aala*, fine," Louise said. She checked the stew. It wasn't ready anyway, the carrots were still hard. From the kitchen, she could hear Flora Jane talking to the babies.

Sinking into a chair, Louise looked out the window. At six o'clock it was pitch black outside, too dark to see the ice fog. Sam was usually home by now. He must be working late. Five of her older children had jobs after school. Weese and Walt, not yet ten, were at the Mayos next door. They'd been over there quite a bit, lately. Then there were the two babies. Ten children in all. How do white women do it? Most white families in Fairbanks have only two or three children. What is their secret?

"Ask them," she had begged her husband. Sam hadn't wanted a big family either. But he couldn't bring himself to ask such a personal question.

Louise sighed. *Where was he?* She looked out the window. A familiar figure approached, but it was her son, John. At fifteen, he was a fierce hockey player in high school.

Louise glanced at the table as she opened the silverware drawer. Sam's place at the end was already set, which surprised her. She must have set it already. Looking at the stew, she realized she'd have to make sure the children didn't eat it all before her husband got home.

She put a lid on the pan and moved it to the back of the black stove. Pulling off her faded bib apron, she raised her voice to be heard over the toddlers' squealing and laughter, "Flora Jane, you and John go ahead and eat, I'm going to take a rest."

"All right, Mom," Flora Jane called back.

✧ ✧ ✧

A week later, Sally Mayo from next door came over with the news that one of Sam's cousins had died. Sally seemed to hear everything as soon as it happened. A few days later, the Harpers went to the funeral at St. Matthews Episcopal Church on First Avenue across from the Chena River. The church was packed. As Louise looked around, she saw the Gassers from the University and George Preston, who managed the NC Company. Both were white families. She spotted her best friend, Rosie Burke, who had come upriver from Nenana. Sitting one pew away were Charlotte and Ben Mayo and Sally and Lee Mayo. Lord, there were a lot of Mayos!

Erinia Callahan, Louise's aunt, who the kids called Grandma Callahan, scooted in next to Louise with a plump sigh. Reaching over, the older woman squeezed Louise's hand. Altoona Brown and Louise's cousin, Lena Chute and her daughter, Ethel, were wedged into the pew behind Erinia and Louise.

"There's almost as many people here as . . . "Lena started to say. Altoona poked her and nodded at the back of Louise's head. ". . . as last time," Lena finished lamely.

After the service, everyone trooped to the hall next door to feast on boiled moosehead soup, rice and moose stew, baked salmon strips, and pickled salmon. Several sheet cakes were accompanied by blueberries preserved with sugar in small wooden kegs and cranberries frozen and stored in sheds since fall.

Around three o'clock, after everyone had stuffed themselves, Louise,

Flora Jane, and rest of the Harper offspring caught rides to the little Clay Street Cemetery on the other end of town. There, with the Mayos and Minooks and other families who had straggled over from the potlatch, they listened to the Episcopal priest talk about Sam's cousin who was going into the ground. A woman Louise hardly remembered. It was then that she realized she didn't remember much of anything. Like, where was her husband? He would have let her know he wasn't coming.

Through the icy air Louise spotted her children scattered among other mourners. How sad they looked. Shifting Donny, who was tied in a blanket against her back, she peered across the cemetery at Sally Mayo. She couldn't tell if Sally was crying. Louise's eyesight wasn't as sharp as it used to be. Not with all the needle work she did at night. Anyway, trying to see through ice fog was like looking through clouds trying to see into heaven. The grainy air muffled sounds, clouded vision, and a person couldn't smell anything but snow.

As she strained to see the priest, she wondered if things seemed so difficult now because she herself was fading . . . disappearing? Into the ice fog? *Kuyh!* Louise took a deep breath and shook herself. Good thing no one could see her thoughts. They'd think she was *Lilun'* (crazy).

Mourners started to leave the cemetery and Louise realized the service was over. Flora Jane touched her arm. "I'll carry Donny, Mom," she said, reaching for the baby.

Louise stretched her back and shoulders, then she and Flora Jane headed toward the street. The younger children ran ahead, their high voices floating across the whitened cemetery like the calls of winter birds.

Feeling lighter, almost buoyant now, Louise looked around the cemetery as if seeing it for the first time—at the frosted birch trees, the old wooden fence.

"Watch where you step, Mom," Flora Jane called back. Louise glanced down. She didn't want to trip over a headstone. That would be bad *Hootlani!* Stepping carefully, she noticed a freshly etched marker set flat in the ground. Something caught her eye.

Leaning over, squinting as she read, she felt a cool wind race up her spine. Then a powerful jolt, as if she was snapping back into herself. It happened so quickly, she fell to her knees in the snow.

Hearing the muffled sound, Flora Jane glanced back. "Mom!" she cried. "What's the matter? Are you all right? Mom!"

But Louise was staring at the marker. Now it was coming back to her.

Fairbanks cemetery with the December sun on the horizon.

With the freezing snow burning her legs, she remembered it all. How the truck had fallen when a jack snapped. How Sam, fearing the baby was underneath, tried to lift the truck. Then he himself had fallen, scaring the wits out of her. And when she couldn't lift him, she'd run for help. But when neighbors carried him inside and laid him on the sofa, he refused to go to the hospital.

"We can't afford it," he kept saying, ". . . and besides, it's nothing."

But unknown to either of them, Sam's ulcer had burst. And within hours peritonitis set in.

Louise looked at the marker for a long time, the ice fog closing in, her lips moving with the words.

SAMUEL HARPER
Born October 13, 1884
Died November 16, 1931

17

Louise's Jobs

FAIRBANKS, 1932

Louise took on extra work after Sam's death.

Sam's unexpected death left his family in debt, with no money for food, house payments, or coal, let alone his burial. For the next eight years, Louise worked as a housekeeper, cook, seamstress, and midwife delivering babies for Native women in Fairbanks.

Usually there were no problems during the births but, to her consternation, Sally Mayo hemorrhaged each time. After the birth of her third daughter, Sally nearly bled to death, and Louise stomped home.

"That's the last time I help her, next time she can go to the hospital!" This was a serious threat. Native women were horrified by hospitals where a white-man-doctor looked at their privates! *Hootlani!*

"We're civilized now," Sam told his wife when Donny was due. "I'll take you to the hospital."

Louise muttered a protest, gritting her teeth through the pain. Connie, who was nine, stood nearby. "Get Sally Mayo, fast!" Louise told her, gasping. Connie ran for Sally. Sally came and Donny was born. Louise sank back on the bed, relieved and looked at her worried husband. *"Now* you can get that white doctor!"

Louise also translated for the Fairbanks courts when Natives accused of a crime were brought in from the villages. She recognized enough of their words, even Yupik, Inupiat, or Aleut, to tell the judge what the accused said, then to tell the confused Native what the court decided.

The older children worked. Flora Jane, carrying a full course-load at the University, worked at the school cafeteria and cleaned faculty houses.

Poor as the Harpers were, they guarded their possessions carefully. One day, Flora Jane was walking into town from the campus, following the Alaska Railroad tracks. The day was unusually warm and the creek looked so inviting she took off her shoes and socks and splashed her hot, aching feet in the water. After a few moments she felt she was being watched. Then, in the trees across the creek, she saw a black bear.

Grabbing her books, Flora Jane flew up the embankment and ran down the track. She got as far as the bridge, when she felt a sharp pain and looked down. She had forgotten her shoes. Muttering every Indian swear word she knew, she set her books on a rock and slowly started back. Bear or no bear, those worn-out oxfords were the only shoes she had.

She saw the bear approach her shoes, sniffing, knee-deep in the creek. The animal was so close she could smell it as she slid cautiously down the bank and grabbed her dusty oxfords. The bear, slurping water, ignored her.

Elsie, Art, and John also worked after school. Elsie worked for the Clarks, a well-to-do white family with two young children. One afternoon, the day before Thanksgiving, Mrs. Clark asked Elsie to dress the turkey. Elsie gave her an odd look and went into the kitchen.

Later, when Elsie was getting ready to leave, Mrs. Clark asked if she had dressed the turkey. "Yes, it's on the table," Elsie said, thinking the customs of these white people were odd.

Puzzled, the woman went into the dining room. In the center of the mahogany table, a large raw turkey wrapped in a pink crocheted baby sweater and boots was resting on a platter. Elsie was almost out the door when Mrs. Clark burst out laughing.

Little work was available during the depression. But John, who had grown into a husky young man, landed a job delivering telegrams for ACS, the Alaska Communications System, which was run by the federal government.

Francis worked in the shipping department at Northern Commercial, and Art went to Anchorage where he found a job driving a truck for the Alaska Road Commission.

The two youngest Harpers faced hard times in their childhood, which coincided with the depression and Second World War. There was so little money that Louise often sent Donny out in weather 30 degrees below or colder to buy a single can of Darigold milk for their mush.

Don's lunch for school was pilot bread and dried fish, or rabbit, or beans and rice. His teacher made the students keep a record of what they ate. Don didn't want to write down pilot bread and dried fish. Who wants to read that? So he copied what the white kids wrote.

Don and Mary occasionally scrounged meals from Doreen Morgan, who was also good for a car ride. The instant she made a move toward her car, the two youngest Harpers were by her side.

One night, when Mary was nine, she accompanied Louise to work, cleaning up after a Masonic meeting and banquet. "There's always food left over," Louise said, knowing her daughter was always hungry. The Masonic Hall overlooked the Chena River and shared space with a mortuary.

It was past midnight before the Masons finished their dinner meeting and Louise began cleaning up.

Mary was wiping dishes when she heard something at the front door, the door her mother had locked after the Masons left.

"What's that?" Mary was jittery anyway, so close to the mortuary.

"Hmmm," Louise said, working faster, soapy water splashing. A stairway to the second floor creaked, and a moment later something scraped the floor above the kitchen.

"Mom," Mary asked, nervously, "Is somebody up there?"

"Just wipe!" Louise's hands were whirling as dishes flew from the dishpan to the rinse water. "And don't drop anything!"

After that night, Mary refused to set foot in the Masonic Hall. Her mother had to persuade Weese or Elsie to keep her company, with promises of delicious leftovers from a white man's banquet.

George Morris was Louise's friend and
companion for many years.

18

Muscatel

Louise and John

No one blamed George Morris when Louise began drinking after Sam died. George was the handsome Japanese/Tsimshian Indian from Cordova whom Louise met some time after Sam passed away. Even if George did manage a notorious bar up the street called the Tamali House.

Louise's drinking began one afternoon when Frank Hite, a neighbor, invited her and Lee and Charlotte Mayo to supper. Frank was a splendid cook and while they were waiting for moose roast and baked potatoes, he poured his guests a strange new drink.

Flora Jane and Louise

"Muscatel," Frank announced, lifting the large bottle. "Fifty cents a gallon!"

Louise had never tasted anything so delicious. As she drank, her melancholy over Sam faded. Soon, she was dancing and laughing and whirling to the music from Frank's wind-up phonograph. She hardly remembered eating that evening, so good and light did she feel.

That night at Frank's house was just the beginning.

Louise and her cousin, Lena, went to the movies once a week, even if they had seen the featured film. For these excursions into town, Louise powdered her nose and put on lipstick. If it was summer, she wore a hat, sometimes with a veil, gloves, leather shoes with heels, and her good navy coat over a rayon print dress. Not to be outdone, Lena, a pretty, small-boned woman, also wore her white-lady clothes.

Often the movie starred Rudolph Valentino, Lena's favorite actor. Like Louise, Lena had learned English listening to people talk. This led to peculiar speech their children (chilrun) called "Indian." "Oh! If only I knew the way to Hollywooot, I'd find Rudolph and have his chilt!" Lena would say dreamily as they came out of the darkened theater onto Second Avenue.

Laughing, they sometimes stopped at the Model Cafe for pie and coffee. More often, they went to the Tamali House, a small, dark bar with a few tables.

Prohibition ended in 1933, but Alaska Natives were forbidden to enter saloons until the late 1940s. Town Marshall Pat O'Connor lived across the street from the Harpers. Before a raid, when he was still a block or so from Tamali House, he'd holler, "Raid, raid, raid!"

Hearing O'Connor's bellow, George yanked a sliding door across the bar, hiding the bottles and glasses, and Native customers tumbled out the back door, George and Louise with them. Running and laughing, they'd come flying into the Harper house, startling Mary and Donny, who hadn't expected to see them until the next day.

George moved in with Louise a year or so after they met. He was every bit as handsome as Sam had been in his younger days. One October, for Louise's birthday, George went to the best jewelry store in Fairbanks and bought her a gold ring with a large opal—her birthstone—surrounded by diamonds. The elegant ring on Louise's broad left hand looked as if it belonged there.

Few recall seeing George Morris drunk, but like so many others in Fairbanks in those days, he was a heavy drinker. He loved Louise's children, especially Mary and Donny and, later, Mike, Weese's first born who lived with Louise. George brought home candy and comics and quietly slipped the children money for the movies at the Empress Theater.

Louise was still doing housework for white families, cleaning public buildings, delivering babies for Native women, and translating at the courthouse. When she wasn't working, she visited friends, which led to drinking.

When Louise drank, she lost her appetite and forgot to cook. George, however, would fix the most amazing meals from old vegetables left outside the grocery store and rice, beans, and rabbit, a staple of the Native diet.

Because George was in the Army, a kind of manservant to the officers, and held odd jobs including tending bar and dressing bodies at the mortuary, his cooking was confined mostly to the weekends. The rest of the time, Mary, nine, and Donny, seven, fended for themselves by sponging off of neighbors.

George loved to bowl. On weekends, he and Louise would have a few beers and "a high ol' time," with Louise flinging that heavy black ball down the lane, any which way. She improved quickly when George showed her how to hold the ball, how many steps to take, and how to release the ball without dropping it. When she saw how serious her Mayo cousins were about bowling, she became downright competitive. The fact was, Louise enjoyed competing, as anyone knew who had raced against her in the Tanana and Nenana sled dog races.

"She's the only woman to win against all those men," Sam used to brag.

If it hadn't been for her heart attack, Louise might never have stopped drinking.

"You've got to stop, Mrs. Harper," Doctor Hale said, peering over his glasses at her in the hospital. "Your heart can't take any more damage."

"You have to quit drinking, Mom, or it will kill you," Flora Jane and Elsie echoed, their dark brows furrowed with worry.

But quitting was slow coming. George softened Louise's grief over Sam, but George worked in a bar, so she drank "to keep him company," as she explained to Lena, who, seldom sober herself, understood perfectly.

Losing dignity disturbed Louise. As she saw it, the Harper name carried a responsibility. A need to maintain dignity, no matter what. Which is why she insisted on being called Mrs. Harper, especially by the neighbor children. How could she be dignified with a bunch of snot-nosed village kids running around screeching, "Louisie!"

Of course, when she was out drinking and laughing, she forgot about it. But the next day, especially if someone was untactful enough to remind her of something embarrassing she'd said or done, she felt bad, disgusted with herself for uttering all those bad words, calling her beloved George a sonofabitch and worse.

In her heart, she knew such behavior betrayed the Harper name.

Weese, now drinking heavily herself, didn't help matters when she brought over a bottle to share with her mother. This made it all the harder for Louise to stay sober and it resulted in a decades-long rift between Flora Jane and Weese.

19

The Decision

FAIRBANKS, 1935

Connie, Elsie and Flora Jane

The old *Deeyninh* stepped outside and closed the door, leaving behind the faint aroma of a recently tanned caribou hide. Through the window, Louise watched him shuffle up the street. She looked at the Mayo's house next door bathed in sunshine but her thoughts were on the old medicine man who came from Tanana by riverboat to see her.

"Young people aren't interested anymore," the *Deeyninh* had told her. They were in her living room that also was her kitchen and dining room. "They're leaving the villages, moving to Fairbanks and Anchorage where there's more opportunity." The lines in his face deepened in the gray light from the window.

Times were changing for Alaska's Native people. Louise and her family felt the change, especially after moving from Nenana to Fairbanks. So many Indians were trying to get jobs in towns now instead of living off the land. Well, that was easy to understand. Nobody got rich living off the land. In truth, people starved when hunting and fishing were bad. She'd seen too many children die from sickness and hunger.

Louise's log cabin was near the Fairbanks courthouse. Her house, lacking a proper foundation, had settled unevenly after years of freezing and thawing that caused the ground to heave. The floor tilted so steeply that when visitors entered, they had to stop themselves from running downhill into the opposite wall.

Her two youngest, Donny and Mary, napped in the bedroom. Seven of her other children were at school in town, and her oldest daughter, Flora Jane was in her senior year at the university.

"I'm getting old," the *Deeyninh* said. "I need someone to take my place." Then he fell silent as if collecting his thoughts.

Accustomed to long pauses in Athabascan conversation, Louise waited patiently. He was leading up to something but she was momentarily distracted by the muskrat trim on his beaded caribou jacket. It reminded her of the moosehide mittens she was making. They needed fur trim before she could take them to Charlie Main's store to sell. She'd have to buy fur scraps from Lucille whose husband had run off with that floozy from Nulato.

The *Deeyninh* leaned forward. "Mrs. Harper, you could do it. You have the gift. But you'd have to work with me," he added, as he settled back on the sofa, "And you know, it takes a few years." His black hair was heavily streaked with white and tied back, tucked beneath his collar. A familiar odor wafted up from his beaded mukluks.

Louise long had been attuned to healing, to the spiritual way of doing things. She sometimes saw things others couldn't. She could sense the presence of someone who had died. She understood the messages of birds, the sounds of wind at night in the trees, strange cloud formations, the way fish ran in a stream. She could make a breeze appear on a still day and she could tell you what your dreams meant.

Like most Athabascans, Louise was sensitive to the rhythms of nature. She knew when these rhythms were interrupted, it was a sign of impending disaster. Like the time the Beluga whale swam into the Yukon River.

At forty-two, Louise knew it took time to learn the ways of a *Deeyninh*. Training was intense. For two or three years she would have no income. A

Deeyninh was paid by families he or she helped, sometimes in food or hides. By tradition, any payment for work Louise performed as an apprentice would go to the elder *Deeyninh*. She understood this, that he needed money for his retirement. Trouble was, after her husband's death, Louise juggled several jobs to support her family.

The man sitting across from her was old and spent. When he stared expectantly at her, Louise took a deep breath. She didn't want to give him an immediate no, as if she didn't respect him enough to consider his offer. This was a powerful *Deeyninh*. She didn't want to get on the wrong side of him.

"I'll have to think about it," she said, carefully. "But I have young children, and I need to work. I want to talk it over with my eldest daughter."

The *Deeyninh* nodded. "Oho," he said. He knew about her responsibilities. He hoped one of her older girls would take the younger children. But out of respect, he said nothing. It was not the Native way to interfere. He got to his feet. "*Kkudaa nidaatsa koonh hoonh tsa adaghoyinee ghaaleedineek,*" he said.

The familiar words, "Goodbye and take good care of yourself," soothed the tired woman. She seldom heard Koyukon anymore. Even her children spoke English. Louise ached for the old words, the old ways, as hard as they had been.

"*Nidaats' i koohn,*" she replied gratefully.

At the window, she looked toward the University of Alaska on a distant high hill. Hadn't Sam warned her against teaching their children Indian beliefs? "I don't want our children growing up believing in superstition," he often reminded her. "We have to learn the white man's ways to get ahead."

Sam had seen white people prosper as Natives struggled to survive. He was convinced his children would have better opportunities if they were properly educated. That meant white schools and moving to Fairbanks.

Brushing a strand of hair from her forehead, Louise frowned. How could she farm out her children to relatives while she moved to Tanana? What would happen to them, to their spirits?

That evening, Flora Jane was washing dishes when Louise told her about the *Deeyninh's* visit. The heavy skillet Flora Jane had been scrubbing slid from her hands into the dishpan and soapy water overflowed.

"He wants you to do WHAT?" Wiping her hands against her apron, Flora Jane sank into a chair and stared at her mother. "Here I am, going to school, trying to make my way in the white man's world, and my own mother wants to become a witch doctor!"

Flora Jane had seen pictures of African witch doctors with bones through

Flora Jane

their noses, plates in their lips, and huge hoops in their ears. She could still hear her white classmates snickering. But she also remembered her mother using spruce to fight colds and coughs, sap to heal cuts, and charcoal to soothe sores when they had been at fish camp, remote from medical help. Once her mother had restored sight to a snow-blind trapper by applying to his eyes pads soaked in the milk of a nursing mother.

She thought of the time her mother was cleaning a narrow-bladed knife she used to drain tubercular infections. When Sam saw what she was doing, he began ranting about Indian medicine. In the middle of his tirade, Louise whirled toward her husband, surprising the bejesus out of him and the children.

"This is a healing tool!" she said, waving the knife in his face, "not super-stition."

Flora Jane sighed. "I know you'd make a good medicine woman, Mom," she said, "but . . . Dad wouldn't like it."

THE DECISION

◇ ◇ ◇

A few days later, Louise sat at the kitchen table with a basket of mending, her daughter's words going around in her head. Of course, Louise knew Sam wouldn't like it. But he wasn't here and he hadn't been around when the children were sick. If it hadn't been for the *Deeyninh*, she was pretty sure, none of their children would be alive.

Yet she knew Sam was right in some ways. The Native people struggled year-round and still went hungry when fishing and hunting were poor. The smallest accident, if a man was laid up for long, could cripple an entire family, sending them into starvation.

Louise sighed. If she refused the *Deeyninh*, she hoped he would accept her decision. He seemed like a good man. Not like that other one years ago, the one who had cursed her unborn baby because she wouldn't sleep with him. "I'm a married woman!" she had protested. But her words meant nothing to him. And then Walty was born, bandy-legged, and looking just like the *Deeyninh*. Worse, Walty had the ambition of a slug.

As she mulled it over, Louise brewed spruce tea and went outside. In June, the lengthening days were sunny and her garden soon would be filled with celery, lettuce, carrots, and a few strawberries. Crouching near the strawberry plants, she reached for her trowel and turned over the dirt.

When an airplane buzzed overhead, she sat back on her heels and watched the silvery shape against the bright sky. In the east, towering white clouds formed mountains and a shape like a wolf. One puffy cloud looked like a man with his arm raised. As she watched the clouds languid movements, her mind wandered.

It was dawning on her that what she was doing—raising her children—was itself a powerful medicine. In a way, she was her family's *Deeyninh*. Louise shoved her trowel into the ground and got to her feet. Flicking dirt from her cotton dress, she knew what she had to do. She would send a message to the *Deeyninh*. She could not accept his offer.

At the door of her house, she paused and looked again at the sky. The wolf cloud had disappeared, but the man-shaped cloud was still easy to see. As she watched, the arms slowly lifted and the figure seemed to reach out as if in blessing, in benediction. In the fragrant air, time disappeared.

Then in a lyrical dance, the white vapor began throwing off bits of itself. Wispy clouds vanished like breath. Until only the sky remained.

Flora Jane

20

The Proposal

Flora Jane (front row left side under banner stripe) and her graduating class at the UA

Flora Jane pulled the scrub brush and pail from the faded linoleum and sat back on her heels, thankful she wouldn't have to scrub floors for a living. Professor Geist's house was one of four faculty homes she cleaned to pay school fees, buy books, and help her mother. She also cleaned for the university president, Dr. Bunnell and his wife, for the Pattys, and for Professor and Mrs. Gasser.

Otto Geist was the only bachelor. Flora Jane knew the stocky forty-year-old German professor was attracted to her. As anyone could tell, he liked Native people, spending many evenings at the Harper home, even when Flora Jane was away.

The previous week, Flora Jane was dusting his bookshelves when he came into the room and sank his sturdy figure down on the sofa.

"Flora Jane," he said, "put that down." He waved dismissively at her dust rag. "Come sit by me." He patted the couch next to him.

"You'll be graduating soon," he began in heavily accented English. "I want you to know I admire your ambition." He took her hand and looked at her. Flora Jane smiled encouragingly.

"But it's hard out there," he continued, "and I want to help you." He paused. This wasn't coming out the way he had hoped. With a deep breath, he plunged ahead. "I want to marry you. I want you to be my wife."

Even though she had somewhat expected this, Flora Jane's stomach flip-flopped. A marriage proposal!

On the practical side, she knew she would have more opportunities as the wife of such a distinguished man. Possibly a teaching position in Fairbanks instead of an outlying village, although that might be unrealistic, her being Indian. But certainly her status in the community would improve.

The trouble was, Otto Geist was almost twice her age. Flora Jane dreamed of romantic love. The professor, with his balding head and short, sturdy figure, wasn't her idea of a handsome husband. She studied his plain, masculine face, the sincerity in his intelligent eyes, and squeezed his hand.

"I'm grateful for your proposal," she said, choosing her words carefully, "but I'm not ready for marriage yet." She paused. "Not for awhile, anyway."

The silence that passed between them was less formal than her words. Still holding her hand, Otto Geist sat back on the sofa. Well, that was that. He knew she didn't love him. Still, he had hoped she would marry for security and position with hope that love would follow.

Flora Jane glanced at the wall clock. She had fifteen minutes to get to her nutrition class. She put away her mop and bucket, slamming the broom closet shut, and grabbed her books. In a few months, if all went well, she would be the first Alaska Native to graduate from the University of Alaska.

Over the past five years, her dark skin and hand-me-down clothes had made her the target of rude stares. When she first came to the campus, she had tried to join in conversations. She had even made friends with two Japanese-American girls in her dorm, but most of the white girls snubbed her.

It wasn't until Aunt Margaret explained it that Flora Jane realized her white classmates and teachers didn't see *her* when they looked at her. They saw the poor Natives on Second Avenue, the drunken Indians and Eskimos on payday.

Even worse were some of the white men. Squaw and savage, they called her. That awful song, *Squaws Along The Yukon*, didn't help. At the soda fountain in the Co-Op Drug Store, when a drunk slipped his hand between her legs, she didn't hesitate. She slammed her heavy English literature textbook into his crotch. *Kee-imph!*

She had to get that degree. It was the only way she could escape the poverty and hardship her mother had suffered. It was the only way she could show people she wasn't just some squaw with a bunch of kids who had to scrub floors for a living.

Flora Jane bit her lip. She didn't want to arrive at class angry, then people really avoided her. Looking up through the dark green spruce, she began climbing the stairs. The steps were built against the wooded hillside in three long sections. As she climbed, sunlight and shadow threw a dancing pattern on the brown steps. Stepping over a rotting board, she thought about the time she almost quit school. *Get a job, get married, give up trying so hard.*

Then she remembered her aunts. Flora Jane met them when she was nine. They taught school in Nenana. How smart they looked in their elegant dresses, silk stockings, and city shoes. When she heard an older girl, a student, call Aunt Margaret "Miss Harper," Flora Jane knew she wanted to be a teacher. *Miss Harper!*

When she started college, her aunts cautioned her about drinking. They showed her how to "nurse" a drink, taking little sips to make it last an entire evening.

"People are watching you," Aunt Marianne said. "If you drink too much, they'll say, 'See, just like an Indian.' "

Aunt Margaret nodded, her curled hair hardly moving. "You can't be too careful."

"Smile, Flora Jane, smile," they added, "people will like you if you smile."

Trudging up the last set of stairs, hoping no one was around, Flora Jane pushed the corners of her mouth toward her cheeks. Her lips stuck, and she had to wiggle her mouth before it finally relaxed.

She'd be twenty-five when she graduated. Two years older than most everyone else, thanks to two bouts of TB. But her aunts kept reminding her, "Better late than never." And important people like President Bunnell, the Gassers, and Lola Tilly—well-respected white citizens who helped run the university—had gone out of their way to tell her how proud they were of her.

Hiking up the stairs with an armload of books was doing further damage to her limp cotton dress. Ignoring thoughts of wrinkles and perspiration stains, she imagined herself dressed like her aunts—in a navy blue suit with spectator shoes, hair "done." Her students saying, "Miss Harper, oh, Miss Harper."

Flora Jane at UA graduation

21

Graduation

Alaska Agricultural College and School of Mines, Fairbanks

Flora Jane lowered the needle of the Singer through the soft velvet and stitched the final seam of her gown. She was going to look terrific tonight or her name was mud. As she urged the fabric under the rapid needle, she saw herself whirling around the floor of the gymnasium, even now being turned into a ballroom by graduating seniors. Her date for the dance was a casual friend, popular and good-looking. Flora Jane felt a secret satisfaction knowing some of the white girls were jealous.

Thank heavens, the rental for her graduation cap and gown was only a few dollars. As it was, she'd saved for months to buy fabric for her gown. She clipped threads, then steamed open the seam at the ironing board, her thoughts moving to her new teaching position.

A few months before, at her aunts' suggestion, Flora Jane sent an application to the federal Bureau of Indian Affairs. Yesterday, she received a letter with a job offer at a BIA school in Chilloco, Oklahoma.

In Oklahoma, temperatures hovered above 100 degrees for weeks on end and insects the size of small birds flew torpidly. The air was rich with rotting vegetation and blooming plants, and people moved and spoke slowly.

Despite the heat, Flora Jane enjoyed her students, most from reservations. She made friends easily among the staff, taking trips with them to Arizona and New Mexico. In Albuquerque, she splurged and bought for thirty-five dollars a gray Navajo rug, never dreaming one day it would be worth thousands. Still, she was homesick. A few years later when a position opened at Eklutna, she returned to Alaska.

Eklutna, a Tanaina Indian village twenty-eight miles northeast of Anchorage, dates back at least 350 years. It is the oldest Athabascan settlement in existence.

In 1924, the government started the Eklutna Vocational School, complete with dormitories, housing for staff and teachers, a warehouse, cannery, meat house, hen house, hog house, and a maintenance shop. Native children from all over Alaska attended the school.

Soon after arriving at Eklutna in the fall in 1937, Flora Jane met Aloysius Bonner, who taught math and science. He had dark red hair, golden-brown eyes, and movie-star-handsome features. He was single, and many of the female students and staff had crushes on him. Some of the girls had even made up a song, singing his unusual first name over and over.

By this time, Flora Jane bore little resemblance to the exhausted college student she had been in run-down shoes and tired dresses. Her black hair curled above her shoulders, and she wore a light dusting of powder, rouge, and a touch of lipstick just inside her lip-line, imitating the fashionably small mouths of English beauties and movie stars.

Sewing most of her wardrobe herself, she wore flattering skirts, dresses, suits, and slacks. She saved her money for "good" shoes, boots, handbag and coat, as her aunts had taught her.

Flora Jane and "Bonner," as she called him, were soon talking and laughing at Eklutna's social gatherings as if they had known one another for years. Even before their first kiss, Flora Jane was a goner. One Saturday, the teachers

Flora Jane teaching at Eklutna

had a picnic at Eklutna Lake. At the end of the day, Flora Jane and Bonner found themselves walking back to the campus together.

When they reached the door to the women's residence, Flora Jane hesitated, then brushed his cheek with a kiss. Bonner bent his head and their lips touched. What began as a polite kiss grew passionate as his lips traveled to her temple, then slowly down her neck. Flora Jane caught her breath and sagged against him. His wool plaid shirt was scratchy against her face and she breathed in the smoky picnic smells caught in his shirt and hair. Swaying together, they moved in two-step through her door.

After a moment, Bonner released her and pulled his shirt over his head. Flora Jane's hands brushed the planes of his chest. His skin was smooth under her tongue and she inhaled his slightly citrus scent. Her hands moved to the waistband of his gabardine slacks, fumbling as she released the buttons and lowered the zipper. His pants fell to his ankles. Kicking off his shoes, he stepped free, the collection of clothes growing around them.

Pausing, Bonner stared at her mouth, then slowly and lightly traced it with his finger. Even as she lifted her face to his touch, she was pulling off her jacket and shirt. Then, in a quick movement, he pushed her onto the bed and pulled off her shoes. His hands went to at the waist of her hiking pants and cotton panties, pulling them down in one motion.

Flora Jane flipped aside the bedspread and lay back on the sheets, cool against the heat of her body. Bonner stretched beside her, his face so close she closed her eyes and breathed him. His satiny skin grew damp with perspiration as their mouths and hands roamed each other's bodies.

Outside, the sky darkened as a breeze picked up and branches began slapping the building. By evening, a tentative sprinkling of rain turned to snow in the first storm of winter.

❖ ❖ ❖

Their times together were so far beyond the groping of the boys at Chemawa, or the awkward thrashing in back seats with college dates, that Flora Jane's heart speeded up at the mere thought of her lover. As she went about her classwork, she pictured herself as Mrs. Bonner, working with him, entertaining at their home, raising a family.

Aunt Margaret and Aunt Marianne had taught Flora Jane about birth control and condoms. Unlike her mother, Flora Jane knew she had a choice. And she wasn't about to get pregnant until she was good and ready.

One Monday, Faith, a rather plain-looking, blue-eyed English teacher, waved her left hand at Flora Jane as she came into the teachers' lounge. Faith was a likable, older woman with a ready smile and she seemed to have no prejudice toward Natives. Smiling at her giddy excitement, Flora Jane looked at Faith's fine-boned hand. A small diamond engagement ring glittered on her finger.

Over the weekend, Faith told her breathlessly, Bonner proposed. As she babbled about a spring wedding, Flora Jane felt something like a dark weight settle over her. Just then, two other teachers entered the lounge and Faith joyously waved her ring at them. She was smiling so much, she was almost pretty.

"I'm going to marry Faith . . . I never meant to hurt you," Bonner told Flora Jane that afternoon. They stood in the shadow of a shed that offered some privacy. Bonner had dreaded this moment, but he owed his lover an explanation. Standing with his hands in his pockets, his gaze flitted across the trees, the ground, the buildings, everywhere but at the Indian woman beside him. Flora Jane's face was puffy from weeping, but now her eyes were dry.

"Did Faith know about us?" Flora Jane could barely talk for her pain. Bonner looked at her and his throat closed.

"She knows we're friends," he said, unable to meet her eyes.

GRADUATION

✧ ✧ ✧

"He wanted fair, blue-eyed children. He didn't want part-Native kids carrying his name," Aunt Marianne said later, with the certainty of one who'd been there.

Flora Jane decided that must be true. Bonner had proclaimed his love so many times, what other reason could there be? Not for the first time, she looked into a mirror with loathing for her dark Athabascan reflection.

Over the next several weeks, Flora Jane sank into the deepest depression she'd felt since leaving Alaska for school in Chemawa, Oregon. After several scorchingly deep cries, she threw herself into tennis and other sports, and managed to finish the school year with a show of friendliness toward Faith and Bonner. When a position opened at the Wrangell Institute in Southeast Alaska, she accepted it, departing Eklutna two days before the Bonner wedding.

✧ ✧ ✧

In the 1930s and 40s, Wrangell Institute was an elegant collection of two-story, white stucco buildings designed by architect Peter Proast of the Sheldon Jackson School in Sitka. In Wrangell, Flora Jane taught girls, ages twelve through eighteen, how to operate a sewing machine, make their own clothes, plan nutritious meals, clean fish, peel and cook beef tongue, bake everything from bread to meatloaf, prepare salads, manage a household, design a floor plan, and care for children.

Wrangell Island was also where Flora Jane met Pete.

Walter "Pete" Petri was a carpenter by trade and an artist by training. Carrying French-Dutch ancestry by way of Illinois, he resembled a bald Bing Crosby, fair and blue-eyed, medium height. Later, some saw in Pete's early photographs a resemblance to Paul Newman. "Something in the attitude," one of the Harpers noted, squinting at a photograph of Pete holding a live bear cub. Pete had a knack for telling stories and jokes. As a carpenter he was a perfectionist. He read everything from *Time* magazine to books on psychic phenomena.

What attracted Flora Jane, however, were his beautiful teeth and generous smile. One night in a darkened movie theater, she reached over and gave his teeth a good yank. To her surprise, they were firmly anchored in his mouth. "They're so perfect, I had to see if they were real," she said, unembarrassed.

Flora Jane and Pete were married in the tiny, white-frame Episcopal Church on a hill in Wrangell on November 17, 1941. She was thirty-one, Pete thirty-two.

Flora Jane and Jan   *Walter (Pete) Petri as a strapping young man.*

"Pete's passionate. He likes to please me," Flora Jane confided to her sisters. Her happy confession was met with startled silence, followed by an Indian all-purpose, *"Hmmmm."*

A year later, the couple moved to Sitka where Flora Jane taught at Mt. Edgecumbe School and Pete worked as a carpenter. They lived in a white-frame duplex on a slight rise near Sheldon Jackson.

Early one February morning in 1943, Flora Jane, nine months pregnant, woke her husband. They made it as far as the Sheldon Jackson infirmary, where Flora Jane gave birth to a five-pound baby girl with fair skin and hazel eyes. They named her Janet Frances after her uncle Francis. When construction work in Sitka slackened, the family moved to the boom town of Anchorage.

One afternoon in November, Flora Jane was pushing her daughter in the buggy-sized, wooden sled Pete had built when she saw Bonner in front of Hewitt's Drugstore on Fourth Avenue. Flora Jane's bruised heart had long since healed and she smiled when she saw his familiar face.

"Flora Jane!" Bonner exclaimed. Giving her a friendly hug, he stepped back to look at her. He was still handsome, though his dark red-brown hair showed a few streaks of silver. On him, it looked good. Over the years, Flora

GRADUATION

Flora Jane with Jan

Jane and Faith had exchanged news in Christmas cards, and Bonner knew his old girlfriend had married. Now, her face had an added expression: Contentment?

"Do you live in Anchorage now?" Flora Jane asked as they caught up on each other's news. Last she'd heard, Bonner and Faith were teaching on the Kuskokwim River.

He shook his head. "Faith and I are in Anchorage for a visit and to get supplies. We're still in Bethel."

His gaze drifted to the sled. The baby was bundled in so many blankets only her face and a bit of pale hair showed. As he took in the fair skin, the infant opened her blue-green eyes and beamed at him. Bonner stared at the child for so long that Flora Jane looked at her baby to see if something was wrong. The infant smiled toothily at her.

Bonner took a breath and straightened up. "You have a beautiful daughter," he said, his smile forced. He looked shaken. Flora Jane smiled, all composure, but a feeling of quiet revenge raced through her. Did he have pictures of his children?, she asked. As Flora Jane murmured appreciatively looking at Bonner's photographs of two toddlers, she was pleased to see that the children took after their mother.

Afterward, as Bonner trudged through the snow to the Post Office, he wondered if Flora Jane knew why he married Faith. How much it had to do with his apprehension that if he married her, they wouldn't have white children. And now his former lover had a hazel-eyed child with red-gold hair.

One morning a few weeks later, Flora Jane was doing laundry in a borrowed wringer washing machine when a letter arrived. She took it to the kitchen table and sat down. Behind her, the kitchen windows had steamed over from the humid air and wet laundry. There was no return address but Flora Jane recognized the handwriting and felt a flutter in her chest as she opened the envelope.

Bonner's elegant script covered two sheets of ivory paper. In a fine scrawl of blue ink, he wrote how happy he had been to see her again.

"I often look back at those days at Eklutna and think of you. Despite the choices we've made, and the course our lives have taken, I will never forget what we had or what we meant to each other. I love you. Bonner."

22

Eklutna Vocational School

Connie, Weese, and Flora Jane.

Childhood measles left Connie deaf in one ear and "cooked off her eyebrows" according to Louise, but the illness did not deter the girl's ambition nor steal away her good looks. Smart in school, Connie was her mother's bill-payer, cook, and babysitter. Compared to plump, talkative, and lively Weese, Connie was nervous, thin, and quiet.

When Louise told her to do something, she did it. "Sweep the floor . . . take the babies around the block . . . run down to the store and get 50 cents worth of soup bones . . . put the rice on . . . stir the soup." Weese, perfectly capable of helping, wouldn't budge. It grated on Sally Mayo when she heard Louise order Connie around, while Weese did nothing.

"Weese nearly died of TB as a baby and your mom like to burst a gusset, doting on her, doing everything to keep her alive," Sally told Flora Jane, who had been at Chemawa when Weese was born. Weese could do no wrong. If Weese got pregnant, Louise would say she was raped. If Weese was falling down drunk, Louise would say some man forced her to drink.

By 1938, times were, if anything, even tougher for the Harpers. That summer, 4-H members from the Eklutna Vocational School came to Fairbanks for a roundup. Connie, a 4-H member, made friends with Susan, a part-Athabascan girl. Connie's cousin, Florence Milligan, also attended the Eklutna school, and the two girls encouraged Connie to apply.

Connie fell ill after her father died and she lost a year of school. Although she was a senior at Fairbanks High School, she wanted to get herself and her younger brother, Walt, who was drinking and getting into trouble, away from Fairbanks.

Getting enough to eat was also a problem. Connie, at 5-foot-3, weighed less than her skinny sister, Flora Jane, and Walt was a bag of bones. When her 4-H friends told her the meals at Eklutna consisted of platters of meat and potatoes and vegetables and fresh bread and milk and all kinds of desserts, Connie was sold.

Josephine Notti, another cousin who attended Eklutna, was standing in the Harper's house, staring wide-eyed at all the children and the list of chores Louise had left for Connie. "You wouldn't have to work this hard at Eklutna," Josephine said, "and they'll help you get into Haskell." She knew Connie had her heart set on becoming a secretary.

Connie wrote to the principal at the Eklutna school. Then she waited. Every day, she stopped by the Post Office to pick up the mail. Louise didn't know what she was up to, and Connie wanted to keep it that way. Then she received a letter from Robert King, the principal. He would be in Fairbanks in a few weeks and he would like to meet with her.

The day of his arrival, Connie hovered in the living room like a nervous bird. Every few minutes, she found herself peering through the window, straightening her dress, and glancing toward the kitchen where Sally Mayo and her mother were visiting.

When Mr. King arrived, Connie opened the door and saw a short, tough-looking fellow with piercing blue eyes who looked like he was assessing the situation. She ushered him inside with a quick look at her mother to make sure she was still deep in conversation.

Mr. King took a seat on the daybed that doubled as a sofa, and came straight to the point.

Eklutna School

"Now, young lady," he said, looking at Connie with his unsettling eyes. "Why do you want to go to Eklutna? You're already enrolled at an accredited school." He frowned at her. "And you know, Eklutna is not accredited."

Connie clasped her hands on her lap to hide her jitters. "There's not enough room here for all of us . . ." she said. She had seen Mr. King look around. He must know he was sitting on someone's bed—a bed covered with a faded, chenille spread, bleached white in places.

She went on to tell him about the year her father died and she had gotten so sick. "There are ten of us living here. Even with everyone helping out, there's not enough food. And it's hard to study at night because of the younger ones. I want my brother, Walty, to come too. He's always getting in trouble and I want to get him away from here."

Mr. King looked around the small room with its worn furniture and at the two Native women in the kitchen. He couldn't remember the last time a student had taken the initiative to apply without adult assistance. He sighed. Ordinarily, it would be in the girl's best interest to stay where she was and graduate. Eklutna was, after all, a vocational school. But clearly, her home situation was troubling. Not to mention what she said about her brother. He leaned forward.

"All right," he said, "now here's what you do. . . ."

When Mr. King finished telling her what train to take, with tickets to be held for her at the station, and when to arrive at Eklutna, he glanced at the women in the kitchen.

"My mother knows nothing about this," Connie said quickly, interpreting his look. His sharp blue eyes flicked back at her.

"Well then, you had better tell her," he said, getting to his feet.

In the kitchen, Louise squinted at the strange white man sitting on the daybed. "Who's that talking to Connie?"

"I think he's from Eklutna." Sally Mayo had seen him at the 4-H Roundup. Louise looked surprised, then worried. Sally picked up a deck of cards and started shuffling.

"Let her go, Louisie," she said. "She does all the work around here and that lazy one doesn't budge." Sally dealt the cards, one for her, one for Louise. "With Connie gone, maybe Weese will do something for a change," she added.

As Sally predicted, Weese now had to cook, clean, and care for the two younger children. The girl lost none of her spunk; if anything, she was more demanding. "I'm going down to the Nordales to babysit, you kids take your bath right now!"

Wary of being smacked, Mary and Don would hop to. At first, Weese took out her resentment over Connie's defection on the two younger children. But as time went on, she became a second mom to them . . . however haphazardly.

23

Mary

Mary (Toots)

Maribeth, or Mary as everyone called her, was five when she fell into the habit of visiting the neighbors at mealtime. Her mother Louise was drinking and rarely cooked. George Morris was a terrific cook but he worked odd hours. So, meals in the little cabin on Fifth Avenue were irregular at best.

Around lunch and again about suppertime, Mary wandered across the street to visit Doreen Morgan, a white woman who once cooked at the roadhouse in McGrath. "I'm here to mop the kitchen floor," Mary would say when Doreen opened the door.

"Well, isn't that nice, but we're just sitting down to eat, maybe you'd like to join us?"

Mary pretended to consider Doreen's offer. "Well, I'll eat first and then I'll mop the floor."

"Isn't that nice?" Doreen would murmur as she filled another plate and Mary squirmed into a chair next to Doreen's young son. Mary alternated offers to mop floors with offers to baby-sit. But she was so young that her way of babysitting meant digging deeper holes in the muddy yard than the babies did with their spoons. Sometimes Mary's little brother, Donny, came with her.

In the summer, when the Morgans went to Circle Hot Springs for a week, they took Donny Harper, who was about the same age as their son. One afternoon, Mary pulled Donny aside. "When you go to Circle Hot Springs, you'll be all by yourself for a whole week. I won't be there with you and you'll be soooo lonesome." It didn't take long to get Donny all worked up, ready to bawl, imagining himself all alone without his big sister.

"Now here's what you do," Mary said when she had him primed. "You go over there and tell Doreen you want me to go with you." Donny frowned in concentration. Then they crossed the street and knocked on Doreen Morgan's door.

"I want Mary to go with me," Donny blurted before Doreen got the door fully open. When she stared at him in astonishment, Donny forgot the rest of what he was supposed to say. Mary bent down next to him, as if to tie a shoelace, and gave him a poke. "Tell her how lonesome you'll be," she hissed.

"I'll be real lonesome if Mary doesn't come," Donny announced loudly. After that Mary went to Circle Hot Springs for a week every summer until she discovered boys.

❖ ❖ ❖

In her early years, Mary was sallow-skinned and bone thin from frequent ailments, including colds, flu, and measles. She had delicate features with large brown eyes, full lips, a slim, straight nose, and a dazzling smile. She played clarinet in the Fairbanks High School band and had several white girl-friends including two sisters, Bonnie and Barbara, whose mother had been a prostitute in Dawson City, Yukon Territory, many years before. Now she was prominent in Fairbanks society.

When Bonnie and Barbara nominated Mary for membership in Rainbow Girls, she was thrilled. But despite the sisters' support, Mary was blackballed at the next Rainbow meeting. She was crushed.

Fourth Avenue in Anchorage in the 1940s

"I'm never going to be friends with a white person again," she declared, her lips trembling.

As she grew older, men were intrigued by her calm manner and they fantasized a concealed, unhurried sensuality. When Mary was seventeen, she married Floyd, a tall, fair-haired soldier stationed at Ladd Field near Fairbanks.

When her sisters and brothers saw Floyd's slick smile and pale, calculating eyes, they said, "Oh, oh."

"Well, maybe it won't turn out so bad," said Flora Jane, who always tried to look on the bright side. Still, no one except Mary held out much hope.

When Floyd was discharged from the service, he took Mary home to Soledad, a small farming community in California. There, she bore a son they named Lloyd. Her husband's relatives, who had migrated west from Arkansas, disliked this timid, too-pretty Indian woman on first sight. They had expected their precious boy to marry a white woman, maybe one with money. Nonetheless, Floyd's parents and sisters, with whom the young couple lived, were pleased to have someone willing to clean the house, cook, and care for the dozen or so children, many of them buck-naked, running around in the sweltering summer heat.

Floyd's buddies and their wives or girlfriends, and their children, all lived together with his family, sharing a couple of houses. Years later, when Mary read about communes, she said, "That was us, the way we lived." Wife swapping was casual. Floyd enjoyed romping with other women in the mish-mash of families and Mary's flat refusal to get friendly with the other husbands put a strain on their marriage. Such high-handed standoffishness also clobbered any hopes she had for making friends in the group.

By now, Floyd was casually cuffing her about, as he might a dog, and Mary was frantic to get away. She wrote to her sister, Elsie, who lived with her husband, Oscar Fast, on a homestead near Anchorage. Mary should get on a train for Seattle, Elsie wrote back. At the Seattle airport, a ticket to get home would be waiting for her.

While Floyd was at work, Mary packed her small, raggedy suitcase. The baby in one arm and suitcase in the other, she walked up the dusty road to catch the bus to Salinas. After buying a train ticket for Seattle, she had $5 in her purse.

In Seattle, she called the airport from the railroad station but no one there knew about her ticket. She found a big chair in the women's room and, after resting awhile, she carried Lloyd back to the telephone.

"No, there's no ticket. Where'd you say you're going? No, sorry, nothing here."

Back in the women's lounge, Mary fed Lloyd and then they dozed in the big chair. A washroom attendant, a middle-aged white woman, had been wiping up around the sinks and refilling toilet paper holders in the stalls. "Are you lost?" Mary's head snapped up and she looked wearily at the attendant.

"My sister in Anchorage was supposed to send a ticket," Mary said. "It's not here, I keep asking but . . ." Lloyd began fretting and Mary patted his bottom. Darn, she was down to the last two diapers. She hadn't thought this trip would take so long.

After Mary made several more trips to the telephone—"Is my ticket here?" "No, not here yet"—the washroom attendant disappeared. When she returned, she was waving an envelope.

"Here," she said, beaming. "Now, you can get on that plane!"

"Oh, thank you!" Mary blurted when she saw the ticket. By golly, Elsie's ticket had finally arrived.

"Now, do you have enough money for a hotel?" The woman's faded blue eyes were serious again. "Because the plane doesn't leave until tomorrow."

Too shy to admit she barely had enough for milk for the baby and a bus ride to the airport, Mary nodded. That night she found a room for two dollars. When she got on the plane for Fairbanks the next day, her stomach was growling and Lloyd was cranky. Several hours later, Mary was surprised when the plane landed in Anchorage and everyone got off. She was supposed to go to Fairbanks, for heaven's sake.

She didn't recognize anyone at the airport, and Elsie had no telephone. Then Mary remembered Elsie's husband worked for the Alaska Railroad. If she could get to the railroad station, Oscar could take her to the homestead when he got off work.

Flat broke now, Mary caught a taxi to downtown Anchorage. "My brother-in-law will pay you, so just wait," she told the cab driver as they pulled up to the station. Inside the building, there was no sign of Oscar.

"He's at the roundhouse," the ticket agent said, pointing through a door on the side of the station. Mary saw the building half a mile down the track and she hesitated. The unpaid cab driver was sitting out there having a cigarette, waiting for his money. Mary chewed her lip. Leaving the cab driver high and dry nagged her . . . but broke is broke. *Desperate times, Desperate measures.* Taking a deep breath, she hitched Lloyd up on her hip, grabbed her old suitcase, and trudged down the tracks. Fine brown dust billowed up, coating her dress and worn shoes.

Four hours later, she and Oscar pulled up in front of the Fast homestead. "Look who I found," he said, smiling when Elsie came out holding their baby, Phyllis. Mary climbed out of the pickup clutching Lloyd. Elsie looked at Mary as if she were a ghost.

"Where'd you come from? How'd you get here?"

"That ticket you sent me was wrong," Mary said. "Why'd you make it to Anchorage?" Mary was sagging from exhaustion. She felt as if she had walked the whole way from California.

"What ticket?" Elsie asked. "I haven't sent it yet, it's still in my purse!"

A week later, Mary and Lloyd boarded the Alaska Railroad for the trip north to Fairbanks. The trip took twelve hours and Elsie had packed a lunch for them of peanut butter and jelly sandwiches, fried chicken, bananas, raisins, and cookies.

In Fairbanks, living with her mother and George in the little house on Fifth Avenue, Mary took the first job she could find. Cleaning two houses a day brought her $10. She also rented a typewriter and practiced her typing. Eventually she found a job in an accountant's office in town and later worked at Ladd Field.

At Ladd, she was impressed by the row after row of women, clacking away on typewriters. When she learned the Teletype operator earned more money than an ordinary typist did, she applied for a position. "Do you know how to run a Teletype?" The manager looked at her dubiously. The young Native woman in front of him didn't look old enough to know much of anything. "Yes sir." Mary's heart started to race. Until then, she had never seen one.

"Where did you learn?" the manager asked.

"I worked at Western Union," Mary lied. *Desperate times, desperate measures.* As soon as she got the job, "on a temporary basis," the manager told her with unflattering reluctance, Mary telephoned a young soldier she had seen servicing a Teletype machine.

"Could somebody come over?" she asked over the phone, her voice low. "There's a little problem here."

The soldier, no taller than Mary, arrived in minutes, intrigued by the fresh young female voice. "I don't know how to work this," Mary said, "but I need the money real bad. How long will it take me to learn it?" The soldier was surprised.

"Two days at least," he said.

"Well, can't this be broken for two days?" Mary said, staring at the foreign-looking machine, "while you teach me?"

So the Teletype was "down" for the next two days while the soldier taught Mary how to run the machine, getting into the rhythm of the clickety-clack to perforate the tape just right.

"You're my best buddy!" she said a few days later, and his round face turned pink.

A secretarial job at Eielson Air Force Base south of town paid even more than she earned as a Teletype operator, but she could tell Mr. Baker, a white man in his late fifties, wasn't crazy about Indians. No one else applied for the position, though, and he needed someone right away.

"You're hired until we find somebody else," he said finally. She'd heard that before. Mary gave him her best smile and decided to make herself indispensable. When she wasn't typing for her two bosses, she was sweeping the floor, straightening and sorting files, and running across the tarmac to the cafeteria to get them coffee.

"We've never had such an eager beaver," Mr. Baker said.

A few months later he gave Mary a raise. He had long since quit looking for a white woman to replace her.

24

The Roadhouse

Circle City Roadhouse.

In Circle City, a roadhouse built during the gold rush still stands overlooking the Yukon River. In the 1930s, the Alaska Road Commission leased it for summer living quarters for its road crews. By 1939, few remained who knew it was haunted.

Louise Harper's cousin, Axinia Callahan Rasmussen, was a petite fifty-seven-year-old widow with an hourglass figure. Every summer the road commission hired Axinia as cook and housekeeper. Her workdays began at 4:30 in the morning, when she baked bread, and ended after 10:30 at night. Always on the lookout for dishwashers, and lonesome for female company, she invited friends and relatives to visit.

Axinia could have invited her cousin by word of mouth but she wanted

to impress Louise, who bragged about her smart kids. So, after fixing break-
fast and cleaning the kitchen and men's sleeping quarters, Axinia struggled
with a letter at the table where she usually made bread, rolls, and pies.

✧ ✧ ✧

A few days later Louise, now forty-seven, had just gotten home from
cleaning the Gasser's house at the university. Sweaty and tired, she dropped
her purse next to the mail on the kitchen table. Francis was sitting at the
other end adding some figures.

"Hey, Mom," he said, looking up.

"Hey," she said back.

Louise sifted through the mail, mostly bills, then she saw Axinia's letter.
Few people she knew wrote, so a letter was like a gift. Louise found a kitchen
knife, slit the flap, and pulled up a chair next to her son. Axinia's penciled
words were large, round, and awkward. As Louise read, she remembered a
delicious noodle, cabbage, and moose dish Axinia once brought to a potlatch
in Rampart.

"Axinia wants me to come visit," Louise murmured as she read. "She's such
a good cook."

✧ ✧ ✧

A week later, on an overcast June morning, Louise and Francis left
Fairbanks in an old pickup he borrowed from his boss. Dust billowed through
missing side windows as they bounced over the Steese Highway. Louise tied
a flowered scarf around her hair, and settled back against the hard seat, smiling. Dust or no dust, she was happy to be going somewhere. Rocks clunked
like gunshots beneath the truck and smaller stones pinged the fenders.

Lifting her voice over the road noise, Louise reminisced to Francis about
relatives who had joined the Circle City gold rush in the 1890s. "In those
days, Circle City was a boom town with about 5,000 people," she said.

Francis shook his head in disbelief. Now the town's year-round population was a few dozen.

The drive from Fairbanks covered 162 miles of rough dirt and gravel
road, and the old pickup seldom went over twenty-five miles an hour. It was
early evening by the time they got to where the dusty road ends abruptly at
the Yukon River. Francis ground the truck to a halt in front of the roadhouse
and jumped out. He carried Louise's bag inside, then disappeared to the outhouse in back. He worked the next day and still had to return to Fairbanks.

Louise climbed gingerly out of the truck, stiff after the long drive, and ran a tongue over her gritty teeth. Stretching the kinks out of her back, she looked at the Yukon, or Big River as Natives called it. Beneath its calm surface swirled undercurrents and eddies that had claimed many lives. In late winter, entire dog teams had been known to disappear through cracks in the ice. Even an occasional moose was swept away. Once a house someone was hauling on runners broke through and vanished. Most of it washed up thirty miles downriver the following spring.

Francis came out of the roadhouse with a sandwich in his hand. "See you in a couple weeks, Mom," he said. At twenty-one, Francis, with his Russian, Irish, and Athabascan blood, had dark hair and eyes, a sensual mouth, and an easy smile. He was slender and, at 5-foot-11, tall for an Athabascan. He climbed into the truck and two Native girls walking by stared after him as he drove off in a swirl of brown dust.

The roadhouse was an L-shaped, two-story log building painted dark red. The main entrance through a small porch led to a saloon. The old plank floor creaked beneath her feet as Louise stepped inside. To the left was a mahogany bar about eight feet long. Behind it, and running the length of the bar, hung an old hazed mirror. Glancing at herself in the glass was like seeing a stranger. Her face was gray with dust and her black hair had loosened into a frazzled bun.

The mirror may have been handsome once but the years it had spent in an abandoned house of ill repute, freezing and thawing with the seasons, had left it in a sorry state. The gilt frame was chipped and separating at the corners and the murky glass rippled like heavy water. As Louise turned away, she thought she saw something move. Looking back into the mirror, she glimpsed a shadowy face.

Doubting her eyes, Louise leaned toward the glass, the buttons of her dress grating on the bar rail. But only her tired face looked back. Behind her reflection she saw a faded, rust-colored curtain. Turning, she saw the curtain blowing gently in an open window.

"Hey Louisie!" Axinia beamed as she hustled across the room toward Louise. Axinia wore a bib apron over a cotton dress and she had put on a little weight. Otherwise, with her olive skin, her dark hair in a bun, and her inquisitive eyes, she hadn't changed.

Without ceremony, Axinia put Louise to work peeling carrots. While they fixed supper for the crew, Axinia told Louise about one of their older uncles who had remarried for the fourth time.

"He's always bragging about his young wife!" she said disgustedly.

"*Anaa da coola*," Louise snorted. "What a lot of talk!" She raised an eyebrow. "What makes that old goat think he can keep up with her?"

They laughed and tackled the next chore, washing the men's towels. Louise admired the white enameled, restaurant-size range. It had a reservoir for heating water and a warming shelf for plates and cups. "It bakes like a dream," Axinia said.

When the men came in for supper, they filled the wash basin with hot water from the reservoir in the range. The men's pants and shirts were covered with road dust. "They're a decent bunch, not like some," Axinia said, shoving a clean skillet into a cupboard. "They're working on the road to Fairbanks. You probably saw them when you drove up."

After drying their hands a final time, the exhausted women left the kitchen and headed through the bar to the staircase leading to the sleeping quarters upstairs. As she followed Axinia, Louise sneaked another look at the mirror. Dark and shining, it looked the same. Then she glimpsed a blurred face under reddish-brown hair, a gold dress, creamy skin. Disbelieving, Louise stopped in mid-tread. Once again, the image disappeared, and the rusty red curtain came back into focus.

"What is it?" Axinia said.

"Nothing," Louise said, puzzled. "Just tired, I guess."

At the top of the stairs, they entered a hall with windows at each end. Although it was nearly midnight, sunlight streamed through the glass. On either side of the hall, rough lumber partitions formed cubicle-sized rooms. Canvas hung from wire stretched across the openings and kerosene lamps hung from ceiling hooks. Axinia had made up an extra bed in one of the cubicles and draped a mosquito net above it. An enameled chamber pot sat beneath the bed and Louise saw a chipped ceramic pitcher and bowl on a rough wooden stand.

"*Basee*," she said gratefully, knowing Axinia still had work to do. With her cousin settled, Axinia hurried back to the kitchen. Louise dropped her bag on the floor and hung her coat on a nail. She pulled off her dress and underclothes, stepped into her cotton nightgown, and climbed onto the hard, lumpy cot. Within minutes she was asleep.

A few minutes later, an outburst of laughter from the bar below woke Louise. She groaned and rolled over on the narrow cot. The saloon's front door slammed and she heard men's voices.

"I'll bet five," a gravelly voice said.

"Hey, barkeep!" a man yelled, "Another whiskey!"

The voices settled into a murmur. She had almost dozed off when some-one yelled, "You're not getting away with that!"

Startled, Louise lifted her head to listen. She heard glass breaking, a clatter of poker chips, and the sounds of a fight. A chair screeched and something heavy crashed to the floor. The gravelly voice yelled, "Let's get outta here!"

Her heart pounding, Louise wondered if she should check on Axinia. Then Louise remembered she'd have to go through the bar to reach the kitchen. No way did she want to be around men who were all liquored up! While she tried to decide what to do, the noises and voices faded.

She must have dozed off again because the next thing she heard were gunshots and a woman's scream. Boots thudded across the barroom floor, and someone yelled, "Oh no, oh no, you shot her!"

Louise lurched up, entangling herself in the mosquito net, then she froze as a mournful keening filled the cubicle. After several minutes, silence descended. Despite her fright, Louise sank into a hard sleep.

After the crew left for work the next morning, Louise and Axinia sat down with their tea. Louise looked at her cousin's tired face.

"Do the men fight like that every night?" Louise didn't think she could take two weeks of it. Axinia looked surprised.

"This bunch doesn't fight at all." Louise stared at her.

"You didn't hear it? All that fighting?" A fleeting frown crossed Axinia's face. She sighed and looked out the window.

"I was hoping that wouldn't happen while you were here." She paused. *"Yiige."* Axinia's voice was so low Louise wasn't sure she'd heard correctly.

"Yiige?" Louise felt her skin prickle.

Axinia looked at her. *"Nasdaetl'ne,"* she added.

Shocked, Louise stared at her. "But it was so real!"

Axinia nodded. "Spirits . . . ghosts fighting."

"You mean all that commotion," Louise blurted, "with guns going off and tables crashing, all that was spirits?" This was worse than she'd thought.

"This crew drinks some," Axinia said, shrugging. "And they play cards, but they don't get rowdy. They work so hard they don't stay up late. Last night, they went to bed, didn't you hear them?" The crew also slept on the second floor. Louise shook her head. All she'd heard was the fight.

Axinia frowned and stared into her cup. "I didn't tell you because not everyone hears it. It happens only now and again." She sighed. "It used to frighten me, but now I'm so tired, I sleep right through the ruckus."

Axinia settled back in her chair. "Boy, it sure scared me first time I heard it . . . must have been five years ago. I asked around, that's how I met this old timer. He was skinny, wore his hair long." Axinia didn't say his name, Louise noticed. He must be dead.

"His hair was white, like snow," Axinia said. "He was the oldest Native in Circle, and he had a deep scar on his face." She chuckled. "You would have liked him, he had so many stories. His voice was odd though, it rattled like old leaves blowing over a river bed." Axinia wasn't usually given to poetic descriptions. Louise was impressed.

"He could talk for hours! But that voice!" Axinia shivered. "Anyway, he said back in the early days there was a lot of drinking and fighting and crooked card games in that bar. And killings. A woman was killed there."

Axinia pushed herself up from the table and began rounding up the ingredients for k'oondzaah, a pudding made from mashed cranberries and pike eggs. The pudding was for her and Louise. For the men, she'd bake a pie. Apple pie, if she had enough apples. Or maybe blackberries.

Louise finished her tea. She couldn't get over it. It so dumbfounded her, she forgot to ask about the mirror. It was bad hootlani to dwell on people who had died. At least Axinia had not said their names. That would summon the spirits for sure!

War, Survival and Remembering

❖ ❖ ❖

*When George moved in with Grandma, Mom was
relieved in a way. She worried less about her mother.
But Mom and Dad seldom mentioned Grandma's boyfriend,
and I sensed shame. Living in sin. Worse, he drank.*

*When Grandma and her daughters were visiting,
I'd hear, "Hey, remember that time . . . ?" and off they'd go,
laughing and talking.*

*They'd reminisce about Mrs. Call, Mom's white boss,
who made my mother bank all her paychecks for college.*

*"That Mrs. Call, she made me save every dime!"
Mom said, happy to have such a friend.*

*If a memory wasn't positive, it wasn't repeated around
children—namely, me. But in Mom's later years, other
words and thoughts slipped out. One afternoon in 1988
we were in Port Angeles, Washington, walking toward the
water and Dad waiting by the car. Looking away from
me, Mom said vaguely, "You know Lucy's daughter is
buried here . . . "*

25

Lucy's Story

Lucy at the funeral of her father, John Minook.

Lucy's calm manner and hint of a smile gave little clue of the rage that she regularly doused with whiskey. The alcohol didn't diminish her anger as much as it stole her energy to hurt herself. When she was in her cups, she thought of her life as a road filled with potholes. Paved streets belonged to other people—white people, mostly.

After Lucy married the Montana gold miner and gave birth to a baby girl, Catherine, she was unable to have more children. Something to do with that time she'd gotten rid of a pregnancy. At least that's what she thought. Lord, that awful stuff she'd drunk had nearly killed her. But if Lucy had only one child, she'd had plenty of "husbands." This was not something she had planned. But after what happened to her daughter, a lot of things changed.

❖ ❖ ❖

Lucy had met Sven in Port Angeles while trying to figure out what to do about Howard, her boyfriend who shot the general store owner in Tanana.

When Sven's job folded and he returned to Montana, she went with him. Sven was thirty-eight and still had all his teeth and hair. A tall, stocky Swede with a gentle manner, his sun-colored hair fascinated Lucy. Sven was race-blind. Lucy was his "little Native doll" and he liked to show her off. Sven had two flaws. First, he was a gold miner who had never had a strike. And when he drank, he had a raging temper, though he was never violent with Lucy.

At twenty, Lucy felt no strong sexual pull toward Sven. Weighing this against his decent nature she decided it wasn't a problem, especially when she had the inspiring and lubricating effects of drink.

A few years later, Catherine was born.

✧ ✧ ✧

At fourteen, Catherine had red hair, pale olive skin, and freckles. Just over 5-foot-3, she stood two inches taller than her mother. Catherine had Lucy's high cheekbones, delicately round chin, and full, upturned lips. Her height and coloring came from her father.

Proud of her daughter's good looks, Lucy remade some of her own dresses, skirts, and jackets to fit the blossoming girl. While not yet the beauty she might become, men and boys already were giving her quick looks, some longer and more calculating than others.

When James Waller, a tall man in his thirties, asked Lucy if her daughter would like to work in his dry goods store after school, Catherine was thrilled. Mr. Waller, who had a family, was courteous to her and her mother when they shopped for fabric and notions in his store. The prospect of earning her own money was exciting. Maybe she could buy new shoes and clothes like her classmates wore. She yearned to be like other girls and to have friends. It didn't help that she was so shy. With all the moving from Montana to Washington, then Alaska, she'd never lived in any one place for long.

After a few weeks at Waller's Dry Goods, Catherine knew the proper place for every bolt of fabric, style of button, and roll of ribbon and lace. Mr. Waller and the customers were friendly and she enjoyed the work.

One day she overheard two customers talking about the girl who had Catherine's job before her. She couldn't make out what they were saying. A few weeks later, Mrs. Habnor, a regular customer, said, "You know of course, that Ellie was in the family way . . ." She raised an eyebrow and gave Catherine a knowing look. Flattered to be taken into the woman's confidence, Catherine tried to look as if she knew what Mrs. Habnor was talking about.

One Saturday, Mr. Waller returned late from lunch. Although it was still early afternoon, he surprised her by flipping the "closed" sign toward the street. "Come on back here," he said, waving his arm at her, his words slurred. "Les you 'n' me do the inventory." Pungent odors of beef stew, beer, and tobacco wafted through the air as he made his way between tables stacked with bolts of fabric.

What happened next was so sudden and so ugly that afterward Catherine tried to pretend it hadn't happened.

"You don't tell anyone 'bout this, you hear?" Mr. Waller's deep voice seemed to be coming from a great distance as his hands continued to drift over her rigid body. He patted her dress awkwardly where he had ripped off the buttons. Catherine's petticoat was bunched up around her waist and stained with blood and something gummy.

"This is a good job for you . . . so let's jus' keep this 'tween ourselves . . ." He belched, his breath ripe, and smiled lopsidedly.

Catherine felt as if she might throw up. Surely she had been ripped apart. *OhMotherMary, the pain, the pain, like knives.* She pushed her torn dress over her knees and tried to climb off the table.

"Let me," Mr. Waller said, his big hands steadying her when she stumbled. Her legs were so rubbery she was surprised she could stand.

On her way home, Catherine moved stiffly. Judging from her awkward gait and tangled hair, anyone would think she had been in an accident. But she saw no one. The tapping of her shoes on the boardwalk broke the evening silence, and the setting sun cast a deep orange-pink glow in the west. But Catherine saw none of it. As she approached her house, she wondered if her mother was home. Usually by early evening, Lucy was having a few drinks, "getting a leg up" she liked to say, before Sven got home.

When Catherine pushed open the door, she knew the house was empty. In the silence, her brain seemed to spasm. Suddenly, all the stupid happiness and hopes and plans she had made were gone. Now she would never have friends or boyfriends. In one afternoon, she had shot right past that girl she had been.

By the time Lucy came home, Catherine decided to say nothing about Mr. Waller. If she didn't talk about it, maybe it wouldn't feel so bad. Maybe it wouldn't happen again. After all, this was the first time she had even seen her boss drunk. But as the days went by, at school or when she was doing some mindless chore, a silent feeling whispered she was wrong.

A few months later, the nausea started. Lucy became suspicious when she found Catherine sick in the outhouse, her face pale and sweaty. When

Catherine told her she had twice missed her monthly "curse," Lucy's alcoholic buzz evaporated. Without thinking, she hauled off and slapped Catherine so hard they both fell on the floor.

"How could you do this?" Lucy screamed, struggling to her feet.

"He made me!" Catherine whimpered. "Mr. Waller made me, he said not to tell."

What Catherine couldn't explain was she had no energy. As if her mouth was too weary to open. The secret weighed her down, took all her strength. It was as if Mr. Waller had claimed her when he put his hands on her and now she couldn't get herself back.

"That sonofabitch," Lucy whispered. "That cocksucking sonofabitch."

Lucy didn't dare tell Sven. She knew her husband would go right out and shoot James Waller, then Sven would go to jail and what good would that do? As she pondered the situation, she went into the kitchen and poured herself a whiskey. It was still morning, but if ever she needed a drink, it was now.

After a moment, Catherine followed and sat tentatively at the table. Despite her mother's reaction, telling her had been a relief, especially now that it was clear Lucy's anger was at Mr. Waller. But as Catherine sat there, avoiding her mother's defeated expression, she could almost hear Mrs. Habnor and the gossip. "Squaws—good for nothing but a roll in the hay . . . and that one, what'd I tell you, that red-haired squaw, she's pregnant, wouldn't you know!"

That night in bed, listening to her mother cry drunkenly, it seemed to Catherine that the walls, the furniture, even the air was filled with her shame.

✧ ✧ ✧

In the shed, Catherine fingered her father's old leather belt. The buckle was bent and he no longer wore it. She wondered if it was long enough. She climbed onto a teetering barrel. When her skirt caught on the barrel's metal rib, she jerked it free, ignoring the ripping sound. The shed was dark, musty, and soundless. In the summer, it crawled with spiders but in November it was merely cold.

Swaying on the barrel, she reached her full height and tossed one end of the belt over the rafter. It dangled above her head. Not long enough. Her shoulders sagged as she stared at it, unaware of her runny nose or tears. The empty black feeling was so overwhelming she found it difficult to move.

Lately, she'd been sick nearly every morning, her belly getting bigger until nothing fit. Even her mother seemed to have lost heart and no longer

Lucy with one of her "husbands"

made her go to school. Catherine no longer went to work. This big stomach was too much to hide and she didn't care what Mr. Waller thought.

Slowly, she climbed down from the wobbly barrel and left the shed, slamming the door behind her. Inside the house, she pulled blouses and dresses and shirts from the dresser and closet. She tied the sleeves together, making sure the knots were tight, fashioning a crude rope. Inside her head, she heard the talking and snickering. She saw people pointing at her, as they pointed at Lucy when she stumbled down the street, a few drinks too many. She heard her mother's deep drawl, "There's no place for us Siwashes."

Catherine grabbed the rope of clothes and walked back to the shed. The sky was gray and the air cool. The sun hardly ever came out, not lately anyway.

That evening, Sven found Catherine in the shed. She was caught up in a gaggle of clothes, the dress skirts covering her head, which was twisted to one side. The yellowed sleeves of long underwear were tight around her neck. The barrel had fallen and rolled out beneath her dangling feet. Sven let out a horrified shout, trying to lift her body. "Lucy! Lucy!" he yelled.

Lucy had been fixing a dinner of pilot bread, halibut, and stewed tomatoes. The alarm in Sven's voice cut through her whiskey haze and she ran outside. "Lucy!" The shed door was partly open. Lucy saw her husband embracing a pile of clothes over his head. Then she saw her daughter's legs.

✧ ✧ ✧

Lucy buried her only child in Port Angeles. In a drunken rage, just as Lucy expected, Sven shot and nearly killed Mr. Waller. Sven went to jail for eight years, and Lucy went on a month-long toot. She grieved for Catherine and was furious with Sven. She had no intention of waiting for him. When a judge in Port Angeles granted Lucy a divorce, she moved to Fairbanks.

In Alaska, harsh winters, poverty, disease, and near starvation made planning for the future a waste of time. Or so most Natives saw it, anyway. This led to a more liberal attitude toward sex, drinking, and spending money. In Tanana and single again, Lucy lead a wild life, "drinkin', dancin' the fandango and having a grand ol' time," as her family recalled.

A few years later, fate took another look a Lucy and decided to give her a break. When it came, she nearly missed it.

One morning after a long night of wild partying, Lucy woke up and was startled to see a strange man snoring next to her. She peered at his pale, whiskered face.

Irritated, she poked him. "Hey," she said. "Hey, you!" She poked harder, her finger making no impression on the man's muscular arm. "YOU!" she said, louder when he didn't budge. "Get outta here!"

The man opened his pale blue eyes and stared at her. He didn't seem to recognize her any more than she did him.

"Nope," he said, finally. "I can't."

Lucy raised her eyebrows. The nerve of this *changh*! "You get outta my bed right now or I'll call the Marshall!" She pushed herself into a sitting position and primly wrapped the blanket around her naked self, all the way to her neck.

Slowly, since he had a walloping hangover, the stranger rolled his head back and forth. "Nope," he repeated, sounding more certain this time. "I can't."

Lucy frowned in exasperation. "Why can't you?"

"Because we're married," the man said politely. He stuck out a big, calloused hand. "I'm Louie Kalloch!"

Contrary to so much that had happened in Lucy's life, the marriage was a good one. Surprising everyone—Lucy most of all.

26

War

Handsome in his uniform, John caught the eye of young women.

Back from Chemawa, John Harper and his brothers made names for themselves in sports. In Fairbanks, they played high school basketball and hockey and joined the Fairbanks Curling Club.

The little Harper house shook as the three oldest boys clumped around in their hockey gear, including chest and face protectors. Arthur, a goalie, wore a helmet and heavy padding. The games were followed by dances at the Moose Hall. After John, Arthur, and Francis left for the game, Elsie, Connie, and Weese would sweep out the front door of the little cabin in a rustle of silky dresses and wafting perfume.

Left behind in the quiet, empty house, Mary and Don often turned to the radio for entertainment, sometimes picking up a station from as far away as San Francisco.

Flora Jane in Seattle, 1941

John

This all changed when the United States entered World War II. Suddenly, it seemed to Mary that everyone—family, friends, people at work—was in a big hurry to go to war. After Francis joined the Army Air Corps and was sent to Europe, Mary sank into depression. To make matters worse, George Morris was snatched out of the Army and taken away because he was half Japanese.

"Ohhh, George's in the internment camp in Tanana . . ." Sally Mayo and Erinia Callahan whispered, their voices low, so as not to disturb Louise who already had a plate full of worry.

Meanwhile, Elsie, Weese, and Connie worked and volunteered in the war effort. Walt joined up and was soon on a boat, where he spent the entire war in and around the Aleutian Islands. John, an Army crew chief, was a flight engineer on the B-17s, B-29s and B-24s. When Arthur enlisted in the Army, he was stationed in Seward, where he managed to get a transfer to Florida and took six months to report to his new post.

Flora Jane and Art.

Laid-back Arthur had masculinity to spare, which netted him a surplus of girlfriends, both white and Native. In Fairbanks one evening, Arthur and his friend Daniel Simpson rented a Model T from Fairbanks U-Drive. While Dan drove with one arm around his girl, Arthur and Josephine Rasmusson were making passionate love in the back seat.

When they came up on a bridge near the Fairbanks Exploration Co., Dan turned the steering wheel too quickly into the curve. The narrow, hard tires skidded on the loose gravel and the Model T went sliding down the bank, flipping over in the water. Amazingly, no one was hurt. Some thought it was due to all the whiskey they'd been drinking.

In the back seat, Arthur and Josephine didn't know what had happened until it was all over.

27

Francis Samuel Harper

FAIRBANKS, 1942

The Ladd Field Midnight Sun

VOLUME III   LADD FIELD, ALASKA, FRIDAY, FEB. 11, 1944   NUMBER 25

EX-LADD FIELD SOLDIER WINS MEDAL

Ladd Field newspaper, Feb. 11, 1944

Francis, or "France," as his sisters called him, was a bombardier in the Army Air Corps during War World II. This was an odd job for their sweetest brother, his sisters agreed.

Before the war, Francis was a shipping clerk at Northern Commercial Co. He had a habit of coming home for lunch, then stretching out on the sofa. Mary, who was eight, would wind up the old Victrola and the music of *Tosca* or Mozart would fill the house while Mary played outside. After awhile the soprano and tenor voices would slow and lurch drunkenly. Back inside Mary would run, her bony arm going round and round as she rewound the Victrola and the faltering voices once again soared, beautiful and true.

Francis enlisted at Ladd Field in January, 1942, and flew seventeen missions over Germany. On the eighteenth, his B-17 was shot down over Bremen. He and his crew parachuted into a field. When Francis untangled himself on the ground, he was surrounded by "a bunch of little kids holding pitchforks," he told his family later.

He spent the rest of the war in a German prison camp. In the camp, one of the other prisoners, an Italian, had a battered trumpet that Francis learned to play, recalling songs his mother had plinked out on her mandolin. Camp was tedious. The soldiers played children's games, even hopscotch. When the Red Cross sent packages of seeds, the prisoners grew gardens.

Francis lost 38 pounds during his twenty months in captivity and like many other prisoners of war he became very weak. "It was painful to see the boys in the showers," he later told a reporter for the *Fairbanks Daily News-Miner*. "Their legs and arms were just pipe stems."

Francis joined several escape attempts, usually involving a tunnel. One tunnel began beneath a latrine. The men carried dirt from their digging out in small amounts and tried to hide it in the yard. Each time they were caught and put in solitary confinement.

"Once, when I was in solitary," Francis told the reporter, "I felt pretty low. The Gestapo was trying to wring information from us, and feeding us only bread and water. I sat in that cell and kept thinking about Fairbanks. To keep from going crazy, I'd picture the whole city, then I'd mentally walk down Wendell to Lacey, trying to remember how each house looked and who lived there."

One day the camp grew strangely still and quiet. Then Francis heard voices speaking English, "I'll go this way and you go that way." A key clattered in his cell door, a man in a U.S. Army uniform stepped inside, and Francis struggled to his feet.

"Are you Francis Harper?" Francis stared at him in shock, then his legs gave way. The man was Forbes Baker Jr., a fellow hockey player from Fairbanks, now part of the rescue team.

In February 1944, while Francis was still in captivity, Louise was presented with his Air Medal with three oak leaf clusters in a ceremony in Fairbanks. He had earned it flying in the European Theater with the Eighth Air Force.

When Francis returned home, he often woke up in the middle of the night screaming. The town rallied around the returning soldiers, especially those who had been prisoners of war. Ruth Barrack, wife of a prominent

| *Francis* | *Francis' wife, Nancy* |

Fairbanks businessman, and Doreen Morgan took a special interest in Francis.

In the months to come, Doreen took her interest a step farther. The Harpers' blonde neighbor wanted Francis in her bed. Soon Doreen and Francis had an affair going. It seemed to help him regain his strength, his family thought.

When Francis's health improved, he returned to work at Northern Commercial Co. and began taking classes at the university. In the summer of 1946, he was managing the NC store in Circle City when two young white women walked in.

"Do you know where we can get something to eat," one asked, a petite blonde with a Texas accent. She and her girlfriend were in Fairbanks to attend college. But classes didn't start for another month, so they'd driven up to Circle.

"No," Francis said slowly, his eyes on the blonde. "There's no place to eat around here." He thought fast. Louise was spending the summer with him in

Circle City and was at home making dinner as they spoke. "But my mother is fixing dinner for a few of us tonight. Why don't you come over?" This is how Nancy, a curvy little former WAC met Francis and Louise. At dinner as most of the Harper family looked on, fascinated by their visitors, Nancy said, "Oh, this is such delicious pork!"

Louise smiled and looked at her son. He cleared his throat. "This is porcupine," he told the two hungry young women.

Nancy bubbled with friendly good nature and Francis found himself laughing, something he hadn't done in a long time. "She's so unusual, she has no prejudice," Louise told her other children. Like other females before her, Nancy fell for Francis and soon was calling him by his initials, FS. In the fall, they signed up for classes and Francis played basketball for the university. Friendly, bright, and with an easy smile, Francis was liked by white and Native students alike.

That winter Francis and Nancy were married in the Episcopal Church and moved into married students housing. But not everyone greeted their marriage with joy.

Doreen was surprisingly bitter about it, and this saddened Louise. After all, Doreen had been good to the Harpers, feeding Donny and Mary when Louise was at an all-time low. Still, Doreen's reaction puzzled the Harpers.

"I don't know what she thought would happen," Louise said, "her being married . . ."

28

Elsie

Elsie and Oscar Fast

In the late 1940s and early '50s, Elsie ran outside waving her dishtowel whenever a small plane flew over. Sometimes the pilots waggled their wings in response before flying on, following the Chugach Range. The mountains glistened white in the winter. In the summer they were a deep purple-blue.

Standing in her dirt-packed yard, watching the silvery speck, Elsie might ask herself, "I wonder where they're going?" Sometimes a neighbor was visiting, but usually she was alone with her toddlers, Phyllis and Richard, and the baby, Esther.

A half-mile toward Anchorage on the Seward Highway, Earl Norris's huskies and malamutes howled morning and evening. Their lonely cries were as familiar as the distant train whistle and the steady buzz of small floatplanes on Lake Spenard and Lake Hood.

Inside the tarpaper shack, the heat was on full blast, summer and winter. A small grease-spattered radio in the kitchen played twenty-four hours a day. Most days, while her husband was at work, the only adult voices Elsie heard were from the radio. Tuned to KFQD, KENI, and sometimes KBYR, she knew by heart every commercial, every song, and every announcer's voice.

There was little traffic since the Fast home was at the end of the narrow, bumpy road connecting their homestead to the highway. Anyone arriving at their house had come to visit, had gotten lost, or was up to no good. Women and children were targets of shifty characters, in Oscar's opinion, and he showed his nervous wife how to load the shotgun. Better for her to have it, he said, even if all she did was hold it. So when he and the truck were gone all day, his wife, with three little children clinging to her spotty housedress, wasn't helpless.

Elsie had wanted to be a beautician. When marriage and children intruded, she gave permanents to friends and relatives in her small, cluttered kitchen. Her aprons and tired house dresses were bleached in spots from Toni Home Permanent spills and she had a stack of thin, faded towels that reeked of permanent and peroxide no matter how often they were washed.

"Suffer for beauty," Elsie would chant in answer to whining and complaints as she twisted pink plastic rods with rubber bands still slippery from old solution. Each curl was so tight, the scalp pulled. Then came the lotion that itched when it dribbled down faces and necks. The ammonia fumes made everyone's eyes burn and water. If Oscar was home, he'd go outside to check on the goats—anything to get away from that damn smell. "Worse 'n cat piss," he'd mutter.

Tudor Road was little more than a dozen wooden survey stakes tied with faded red rags and jabbed in the muskeg, vaguely pointing the way east toward the Chugach Range. Elsie told her children that someday Tudor road would cross Seward Highway and go west toward the airport. Residents in the "Fast Subdivision," home to about six families, tried to imagine Tudor Road going any direction at all as they stood in the swamp, burning their trash in fifty-gallon drums that they later overturned for land fill. In the summer, they had to watch like hawks to keep the peatmoss from catching fire. Once a peatmoss fire got going, it was holy-hell to put out.

A narrow path, bony with roots, connected Elsie and Oscar's house with Flora Jane's place. Flora Jane and her husband, Pete, had bought an acre of

Phyllis, Elsie, and Oscar Fast

the Fast homestead and hauled a small house that Pete built from Third Avenue in Anchorage. They made $45 a month payments to Oscar and Elsie for the next five or so years.

Elsie and Flora Jane beat a path through the weeds with shovels and axes and by stomping their feet in heavy winter boots. They laid down scrap lumber across the wet places and over ditches. Even so, anyone using the lumpy path kept their eyes glued to the ground for fear of tripping over roots or falling off the wobbly boards and winding up on their butts in the mosquito-infested swamp.

Of all the Harper daughters, Elsie and Weese most loved to eat, and it showed. Where Weese drank herself silly in her early years, and enjoyed a number of "husbands," Elsie had one husband and for a long time she limited her drinking to an occasional cocktail. Like mama bears, both had a quick temper and dispensed discipline among their young with lightning speed and a powerful hand.

"Ohhhh, that Elsie, what a temper!" Pete would say, shaking his head and hiding behind a book whenever his wife and Elsie got into one of their arguments—Flora Jane tight-lipped and glinty eyed, Elsie yelling and slamming doors, each forbidding her children from entering the other's home. Within a week or so, after a little tippy-toeing around, the sisters made up and soon all was back to normal—until the next time.

The sisters' families were connected to the four other families, all of whom had bought a piece of the homestead, with a government-surplus telephone system Oscar had bought from the Alaska Railroad. Flora Jane and Elsie called it a "rabbit line" after a telephone system installed by soldiers along the Yukon River when they were children. The phone was for gossip mostly and dealing with the occasional emergency, especially in the late 1940s and early '50s when storms could blow snowdrifts ten to fifteen feet high overnight.

Oscar was English-born by way of Nebraska, gangly and outgoing. He had a special affinity for his youngest child, Esther. As soon as he came home from work, she climbed all over his 6-foot-3 frame, clinging to her father like a trailing sweet pea, both of them laughing. "Thank God for Oscar!" relatives said, since Elsie was impatient with all that lovey-dovey stuff.

Neighborhood children learned to be wary of playing with the Fast kids when Oscar was home. It wasn't unusual to see him grab a chicken with his large, rawboned hands, haul it to the chopping block, and *whack!* The small head with its orange beak squawked on the stump while the body raced around the yard, spraying blood over dusty fireweed. When Elsie told them what was for dinner, Phyllis and Richard played down by the cow pasture, well away from the chopping block.

One afternoon, two-year-old Esther was playing in the yard when Oscar, thinking all the children were in the house, beheaded a chicken for the family's dinner. As the frantic body ran in circles, Esther tried to get out of the way. But no matter which way she ran, the headless chicken was right behind her, feathers flying, wrinkled orange legs and claws pounding the dirt. And behind them both came Oscar, trying to reach his screaming daughter. Finally, his long arms lifted her out of the path of headless bird.

Pete, Flora Jane, and Jan

Before Thanksgiving one year, Oscar told his wife they would have to eat Beauregard. Property taxes were due and they were pinching every cent, including grocery money. When Flora Jane and Pete, who usually spent Thanksgiving with the Fasts, learned what was for dinner, they made other plans.

Richard, who was five, had spent many hours talking to the bull through the fence, watching in fascination as he ate, flared his nostrils, switched his tail, snorted, and rolled his eyes at the cows.

On Thanksgiving, Beauregard, husband of the cows and father of several calves, was a platter of dark meat in the center of the table. Richard and Phyllis sat red-eyed, a hiccup away from hysterics. Esther, sensing something bad, took her cue from her brother and sister, prepared to cry instantly.

Usually the sight of weepy children incensed Elsie into yelling, "Let's see some smiles around here!" But she was silent as she filled a plate with yams, carried wobbly green Jell-O to the table, and spooned Del Monte carrots onto scarred plates. Taking her seat at the end of the table opposite her husband, she bowed her head, and seven-year-old Phyllis croaked out, "Bless this food to our use and us to Thy service, Amen."

In 1954, at age forty-three, Oscar fell over dead while he and Elsie, drenched in *Evening in Paris*, vigorously worked on making another child. An autopsy revealed lungs coated with coal dust and a brain tumor. The tumor, everyone agreed, explained the violent headaches that would sneak up on Oscar and hit him like a baseball bat.

"Twenty years working for the railroad, look what it got him!" Flora Jane's husband muttered, his cigar wafting sourly through the funeral parlor. Friends, relatives, Alaska Railroad co-workers, VFW comrades, and clergy surrounded Elsie and the kids.

Oscar left no will, and the homestead fell into the eager hands of lawyers and a court system suspicious of Natives. "They think she's going to take the money and run—leave her children orphans!" Flora Jane raged to her co-workers at the Loussac Library. Her ulcer was eating a hole in her gullet with all the worrying, she told her husband.

Before Oscar's death, the family had a steady, if small, year-round income. Now, the Episcopal Church and Salvation Army pitched in with money, clothing, food, and moral support. Elsie's sisters prayed long and hard, giving God all manner of suggestions.

"Please hurry up those GD lawyers," was Flora Jane's favorite when she was rushed and didn't have time to think of something more religious.

"No, no," Pete protested. "Don't tell God what to do! Just ask Him to help her in the best possible way."

Flora Jane nodded, appreciating his advice. But, with a lifetime of boss-ing—as a teacher, stand-in mother, club president, and drill team leader—her impatience got in the way.

In any case, Elsie and the kids had several impoverished years before the court permitted her to sell even one acre. "Land rich and cash poor" was the litany of her friends and relatives.

Oscar was gone, but the family car was parked in the yard, surrounded by chickens, geese, ducks, goats, and weeds. In the midst of her tears, Elsie had to learn to drive. She lasted through two driving lessons with a valiant neigh-bor. "Doing his Christian duty," Flora Jane observed.

It was a traumatic experience for everyone. Elsie's car acquired dents, dings, and deep scratches. "Character lines," Elsie called them as she bombed around town, driving mostly by feel. She had no sense of the perimeter of the '48 Plymouth as she lumbered over curbs mashing fenders and bumpers, and shattering many a headlight and taillight. But one look at the heavyset woman with the determined expression convinced even the most irritated motorist that maybe it wasn't so bad after all. "It's good for her to learn to drive," said Flora Jane, herself a cautious driver.

Pete laughed, seeing humor in most things. Nevertheless, he looked apprehensive when Elsie drove by on her way home.

"You never know if she's going to stay on the road," he said, chewing on his cigar. "If something catches her attention, before you know it the car's headed that way, road or no." More curious than her assorted cats, Elsie once pulled over when she spotted a highway patrol car partly concealed behind bushes at the corner of Seward Highway and Tudor, by then a two-lane, gravel road. Elsie rolled down her window, and hollered, "Whatcha doing?" Startled, the patrolman hunkered behind his steering wheel.

"Get outta here!" he growled, waving his hand, motioning her on. Elsie looked from him to the highway, then back again.

"What're you doing back there in the bushes?"

The cop glared at her. "Go on, beat it!" Elsie turned off her ignition and settled in with a look of expectation on her face. This was better than *Secret Storm*, the TV soap she watched every day at 3:30. Some minutes later, Rose Larson, a neighbor, drove up in her pickup.

"Hey, Elsie," she shouted, "You having car trouble?"

Elsie shook her head, her eyes bright. "Nope, I'm waiting." She motioned

Flora Jane and Jan

to the patrol car behind the bushes. "To see if he's gonna nab anyone." Rose leaned through the pickup's side window and squinted at the patrol car through coke bottle glasses. Pink curlers and a nylon chiffon scarf hid her black hair.

With a big sigh, the cop pulled himself erect behind the steering wheel. "I'm watching for speeding cars," he said, disgustedly. Starting the car, he stomped on the gas. The patrol car shot out from behind the bushes, spewing gravel as it lurched across the shoulder onto Seward highway.

When Elsie told Pete about the speed trap, he laughed until tears came. "That Elsie!" Flora Jane said, worried. "What *will* she do next!"

One day in May, the State Troopers drove out to see Elsie. A little later, in a flurry of nerves, she called Flora Jane. The following Saturday, instead of walking over to the Fasts to see how they were doing as had been his custom since Oscar's death, Pete stayed home.

A few years earlier, Oscar had bought a boxcar from the Alaska Railroad. He hauled it home to store feed and farm equipment. Unknown to Elsie, Frank Westerly, husband of her best friend, along with his two oldest sons and a few cohorts, had robbed the Alaska Railroad. Westerly stashed the loot, $15,000 in cash, beneath bales of hay and sacks of chicken feed in the boxcar.

A sandy-haired white man, Westerly had smiling eyes and smooth features that appealed to women. He had twice done time for burglary and his two older sons were showing similar promise.

Cate, his petite Athabascan wife, worked steadily at a number of cleaning jobs. She had a tired, once-pretty face, and she wore worry lines the way some women wear lipstick—straight across and deep.

After Oscar's death, Frank, his buddies and sons got into the habit of dropping by the Fast homestead, where they'd drink themselves silly, forcing the Fast kids to hide out somewhere until the men were gone. Oscar had always run Frank off but, in her grief, Elsie had no energy. Besides, how could she make them leave? They knew she wouldn't shoot her best friend's husband or sons.

A few weeks earlier, Pete had wandered over to check them out. Pete weighed 145 pounds, was bald and middle-aged. He knew as soon as he saw the motley bunch, they'd beat him to a pulp if he so much as hinted they get the hell out and leave his sister-in-law alone.

The Saturday Elsie warned Pete to stay home, Frank and his cronies and sons were hanging around the boxcar, drinking beer. While they were talking about what they'd do with their haul, a dozen FBI agents in suits and State Troopers in uniforms erupted into Elsie's chicken yard, waving guns. No shots were fired as the crooks slowly raised their hands.

Elsie couldn't believe all that money had been hidden in her boxcar. "Lord a goshen," she said to Flora Jane. "Cate had no idea Frank robbed the railroad."

"Humph!" snorted Pete, chewing on his cigar. He'd known all along those sonsabitches were up to no good. They had that jail-bird look.

"And those boys of hers, back in prison," Elsie went on, her own troubles temporarily forgotten. "All Frank and those sons ever caused her was grief . . . "

"Thank the good Lord, that's over!" Flora Jane breathed when Elsie left. Now Flora Jane could quit worrying about that, and go back to telling God what to do about her sister's land.

As Elsie battled in the courts for the right to sell some acreage, "talking to all those high-priced lawyers" gave her a confidence unusual for any woman at the time, let alone a Native woman. A few years earlier, Anchorage's bars and restaurants had been off limits to Alaska Natives. The stink of prejudice continued to intimidate Natives, who often were shy around whites, anyway. Elsie wasn't shy and she'd be damned if she'd be intimidated. After a few years, most people in Anchorage knew who she was.

When Gov. Bill Egan passed through Anchorage International Airport, he'd wave and call out, "Hiya Elsie, how you doing?" From the VFW tourist information booth where she volunteered, Elsie would call back, "Hiya, Bill."

After years of legal hassle, she was given the go-ahead to sell a few lots each year. She promptly moved her family into a tract house in Wickersham Park off Lake Otis Road. Her plans to tear down the old, rat-infested shack Oscar had built were interrupted when a family asked to rent it. Elsie talked to her lawyer, John Hellenthal, who had the family sign a waiver "in case the roof fell in." The new tenants began paying rent. "Elsie's a landlord!" Pete and Flora Jane said in amazement.

29

The House in Spenard

ANCHORAGE, 1964–1970S

Don Harper

Don Harper slid across the cracked vinyl seat, jammed a key in the ignition, and threw the gearshift into reverse. He stomped on the gas and the truck careened onto 32nd Avenue, kicking up rocks and dirt. He shifted into third and glanced at his watch. Two o'clock in the morning. If it hadn't been for his scare, he'd be in bed.

To the east of Anchorage, the sun over the Chugach Range glazed Alaska's largest town in silver-pink light. Early in the morning, the May air was especially fresh, sweet, and balmy.

One hand on the steering wheel, Don pawed through the glove compartment for his sunglasses. His fright was already fading, like something sliding under water. Even so, he kept driving, turning off Seward Highway onto Tudor, then right onto Lake Otis and another into Wickersham Park. With a sigh, he pulled up in front of a white frame house. The green trim was peeling, definitely ready for a paint job.

Don banged on the back door. After a moment, he heard his fifteen-year-old niece call, "Who is it?"

"It's me, Don!" Then the door rattled as his sister Elsie slid back the latch.

"What in Sam Hill are you doing here?" Elsie clutched a flowered house-coat around her hefty figure as Don stepped inside. "Criminny, it's two in the morning, you like to scare me out of my wits!" Pink curlers pulled her hair so tight her scalp showed. Don silently thanked heaven he was a man. He couldn't imagine putting up with all that paraphernalia.

"Sorry, Elsie . . ." Don said. For a moment he was silent. He had been in such a hurry he hadn't thought of how to begin.

"Are you in trouble?" Elsie turned the burner on under the coffeepot. Activity at this unholy hour had set her heart racing and she sat down heavily at the kitchen table. Don pulled out a chair across from her. "So what is it, what's wrong?"

"I think my house is haunted," he blurted. Elsie's glasses were in the bedroom and she had to squint at her younger brother to see if he was joking.

"What happened?"

Don twirled the sugar bowl, to keep his hands from shaking. "There's something in my house," he said, releasing the sugar bowl. "First, it was a sound like dog's toenails on linoleum. Then I thought it was power lines hitting the house. But after awhile I knew it was coming from inside.

"Pretty soon, I'd hear it again, from the kitchen. I'd run in there, switch on the lights, look all around . . ." He shrugged. "Nothing. Everytime I'd hear it, I'd check the back door, make sure it was locked . . . then I'd go back to watching TV. Pretty soon, I'd hear it again, taptaptap."

"When did all this start?" Elsie shivered, pulling her robe closer.

"Oh hell, just after I moved in . . ." Don sighed. "But tonight, I went to bed and left the radio on. Anyway, I'm just closing my eyes when I see this thing by the door. It's all hazy and gray, but it looks like an old woman . . . Jeez, I couldn't move! The next thing I know, she's on top of me!" His voice cracked. He was quiet for so long that Elsie stirred impatiently.

"So what happened?" On the stove behind them, the coffee burbled, and the smell of Hills Bros. filled the kitchen.

"It landed on me!" Don's voice rose. "I felt like I was suffocating! Then it slid off the other side of the bed." Speechless, Esther and Elsie stared at his drawn face.

"Claustrophobia," ventured Esther. She was on the C's in her vocabulary book.

"Yeah, something like that." Don stared at his coffee. "As soon as I could move, I looked under the bed, in the closet. Nothing. Finally, I moved to the couch. My head was resting on the arm and I'm just dropping off when, whack! Right by my head, like somebody'd smacked the arm. God, I flew off that couch!"

Elsie felt twitchy and glanced at her watch. She'd have to wait six hours before calling Fairbanks to tell her mother. "This happened tonight?"

"Yeah! Just a little while ago. My heart's still going a mile a minute."

"Mom, I want to stay over there." Esther said.

"Yeah, come on," Don joked, nervously. "You guys camp out there and I'll stay here."

Don had grown up surrounded by spirit talk, but he'd quickly learned from his white teachers at Mount Edgecombe and Eklutna that spirits and ghosts were just the superstitious beliefs of ignorant people. Talking about them would label him a hick or a drunk.

Don was puzzled by this ghost business. Even when he'd been married and drinking, he had never seen spirit stuff. Hell, sometimes he didn't even see what was in front of him! He sighed, and wondered what his ex-wife would think. Or his daughter, all of fifteen now.

For the next several days, Don went about his daily routine. In the morning, he got in line at the Electricians' Union Hall. Jobs were few, but at least his name was moving up the list. After supper, he bowled for the Alaska Native Service team. When he got home around 10:30, he stretched out on the couch to watch television. Almost every night, he heard the "taptaptap."

A couple of times, he thought he'd seen something move. His ghost house, as he now called it, belonged to friends, Marge and Bill. It had been empty awhile and they let him stay for just enough rent to cover utilities. Until Don went to work, he didn't have enough money for all the deposits a new place required.

A few days later, Elsie called. "Don, Mom's here and she's brought a friend from Galena. They're real interested in your ghost."

When Don arrived, his mother was still in her travel outfit—a brown cotton print dress under a hand-knit cardigan, heavy stockings, thick-soled brown oxfords, and a hair net over her bun. He could smell the coal of her stove, the Coty face powder, and Jergens lotion.

Next to her was an old Athabascan woman with fragile bones, wrinkled

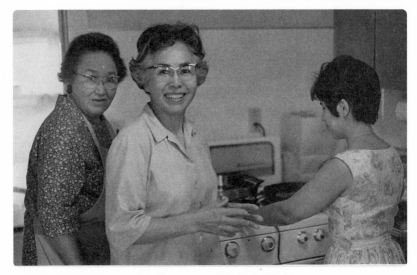

Elsie, Flora Jane, and Shirley Paddock

skin and sorry teeth. She looked about ninety. "Ruth's come to Anchorage to get married," Elsie said, stunning Don into silence. "She and Mom want to hear your story." Pulling him aside, Elsie whispered, "Ruth's a powerful spirit woman."

The old woman spoke only Koyukon but she hung onto Don's every word. When he finished, she and Louise talked back and forth, and Don caught a soft vowel, a glottal, and the hissing sounds he remembered from childhood.

Finally, with Louise translating, Ruth said, "A long time ago, a woman died in your house. A white woman. She had the smoking sickness. Lucky Strike cigarettes all around." She paused, as if inhaling the distant smoke. "She feels it's her house. Her spirit resents you being there. So this is what you do—fix a meal and a pot of tea. Put it at the end of the stove." She paused. "If you show her you're friendly, maybe she'll stop bothering you."

Don nodded, politely. *Oh boy, now I'm supposed to feed a ghost.*

On the way home, he realized he had forgotten to tell the old woman about the odor of cigarettes that appeared with the taptaptap. He hadn't smoked in years and the odor had mystified him. Another thing, what if Marge or someone came over and saw this spirit meal sitting on the stove? They'd think he'd fallen off the wagon.

For several days, Don did nothing. To his relief, he didn't see the gray figure again, but the nightly taptaptap and wafting cigarette smoke continued. "It's driving me up the wall!" he complained to his sister over the phone.

"Did you fix a meal like Ruth said?" Elsie asked. Don sighed.

That afternoon, he heated some leftover beef stew and filled the kettle for tea. He was dishing up the stew when the phone rang. The dispatcher at the union hall told him that starting Monday he had a job on the new school.

Putting down the phone, Don grinned at the empty kitchen. Now he could move! Then he caught sight of the stew. Oh hell, why not? It would take awhile to find a new place anyway.

While he was making tea for the ghost, he was startled by a knock on the back door and spilled water on the counter. Through the screen, he saw Marge's round face and yellow hair. Oh boy.

"Come on in," he said, grabbing a roll of paper towels.

"Hey Don, how're you doing?" Marge pushed open the door and stepped into the kitchen.

"Listen, Don . . ." she began. She seemed nervous, even apologetic. "I've got some people who've come up for the earthquake. And I've promised them this place." Ever since the Good Friday earthquake in March, swarms of engineers and seismic specialists, lured by federal disaster money, had been pouring into the state. Marge's curious eyes settled briefly on the stew and mug of tea. Don wiped up the spilled water.

"Okay," he said. "That's fine . . ." He was a little dizzy with all this sudden activity. He was finally getting what he wanted, but after waiting for so long, he was rusty at having to think faster.

"Yeah, really," he said, when Marge still looked concerned. "I just got a call from the union. I'm starting work next week. And I might know someone who's got a place to rent."

Marge brightened. "Oh, wonderful," she breathed. She glanced at the stew, congealing on the stove. "Now, I don't want to rush you," she said, "but how soon can you move out?"

"Hell, Marge," Don said, smiling brightly, "I can be out of here tomorrow."

"Really?" Her eyebrows rose.

"Why, sure!" He was feeling lighter by the minute. So what if he had to sleep a night or two in his pick-up or in Elsie's basement?

At six o'clock the next morning, Don rolled out of bed and finished loading his television and clothes into his pickup. Then, he started cleaning. By five-thirty that evening, the house gleamed. Even the tired linoleum had sheen of fresh wax.

Don was admiring his work when Marge came up the steps with a woman. "Wow, this place is spotless!" Marge wasn't much of a housekeeper, and she smiled. A small blonde woman peered around her.

"Oh!" she blurted. "This is darling!" Her name was Dot. Her husband had a contract to rebuild Seward's dock, which was destroyed by the tidal wave that followed the quake. "And on weekends, my husband can come from Seward . . ." Dot said. The two women left to check out the rest of the house.

"Marge, the keys are on the table," Don called out. "We're all square, I'm leaving."

"See you, Don," she said.

"Yeah, see you later, bye." As Don headed for his pickup, he took a look at the lady's car, a spanking new 1964 Chevy.

✧ ✧ ✧

One night, several months later, Don decided to treat himself to a cook-it-yourself steak at the Chef's Inn after work. The bar-top dancing hadn't started yet, so he figured it was safe to eat at the piano bar without someone's foot landing in his food. When he left at nine o'clock, the sun was still high. It was not a great TV night, and Don turned the pickup toward 33rd Avenue.

This was not his first drive-by. The woman's Chevy was followed a few months later by an older Cadillac, then a five-year-old green Pontiac. Tonight, a "For Sale" sign stood in the yard.

✧ ✧ ✧

In the 1970s, Don went to work on the trans-Alaska Pipeline. Guaranteed time off, called Rest and Relaxation, or R&R, was written into the labor contract to compensate for the "seven 12s," schedules calling for working seven days a week, 12 hours a day. Don alternated his Las Vegas trips with more frugal visits to Anchorage.

During an Anchorage visit, he decided to drive by the ghost house, remembering to turn at the laundromat on 33rd.

The house was now painted bubblegum pink and a neon sign anchored to the roof screamed "TWIN PEAKS TOPLESS, Happy Hour Every Night." Flashing pink neon outlined two breasts. Three police cruisers were in the driveway.

Don stared at the scene awhile before turning around and heading back to his motel. He wondered how his ghost was getting along with the new tenants.

30

Visitors

Louise holding grandchild, Mike Harper.

Louise Harper buttoned her dress, finished wrapping her hair in a nearly invisible net, and walked purposefully into her daughter's living room. There, her stride faltered. She looked around. She came in here for *something*, but what? Seeing George just now made her forget. His presence was always a comfort, even all these years after his death. But now she'd forgotten what she was looking for.

Oh, that was it. A needle, that's what she needed.

Louise's vision was so poor, even after cataract surgery, that she no longer did bead work. But for heavensakes she should be able to sew up a hem in her dress. Even a bad sewing job was better than having it trail around her ankles. Like she was some drunk Indian slouching along Second Avenue. Louise snorted at the memory of such behavior and made her way to the chest of drawers where Weese kept her sewing things.

Funny, she thought as she threaded a large-eyed needle. She didn't recall seeing Sam after he had died. Oh, she had sensed his presence a time or two. But she hadn't *seen* him. Maybe she was too filled with grief. Or maybe she was too young then. She didn't want to think it was because she'd been drunk. *That* she didn't want to think about. She had managed to slow down her drinking after several more hospital visits and with her doctor and daughters nagging her. But what had truly frightened her and made her quit was George dying of heart failure and her own health being so wobbly.

Lordy, after Sam died, she used to plink on her mandolin and sing those sad songs and just drive her daughters nuts. "Mom, you want to go down to the Model Cafe for pie and coffee?" they'd ask, their faces hopeful. She'd stop, look at them, and shake her head. Then she'd take a deep breath, "I was dancing with my loved one the night they were playing the beautiful Tennessee waltz . . ." And here she sometimes forgot the words ". . . when an old friend I happened to seeeee, I introduced her to my loved one . . . and while they were dancing . . ."

"Mom, you want to go to a movie?" Flora Jane, or Elsie, or Connie would ask, their voices plaintive.

"NO!" she'd yell, glaring at her girls. Then, taking another breath, trying to remember where she'd left off, "I rememburrrr the night of the Tennessee Waltz, when my friend stole my . . ."

"Mom? You want . . ."

"Oh all right!" And she'd dump her mandolin on the floor with a thud. Then she'd get her coat, stuffing her arms in the sleeves, her dress bunching up, her daughters trailing after her. Put on some lipstick, Mom, comb your hair. Connie waving a rat-tailed comb. Mom, Mom . . . and off they'd go to the movies or to window shop, or for pie and coffee at the Model Cafe. Anything just to get away from that mandolin and mournful singing.

She was older now and not feeling so good, maybe that's why she was seeing George so often. And sometimes her mother and father and Sam too. Even Jenny Harper, Sam's mother. Maybe they were getting ready for her. The idea didn't especially bother her. Her heart hurt, her hearing was nearly gone, and her eyesight presented vague images at best. Not to mention her stiff joints and the depression that followed her around like a hungry dog.

Oh, she enjoyed her children and their children, so many in college now. Conversations with her sons and daughters and the energy of her grandchildren kept her alive when so many of her friends were gone. When she was younger she hadn't wanted such a big family. Four would have been nice. But ten! Still, she loved every one of them, even Walty, cursed from the time he was inside her.

She remembered Sam's reaction when she was pregnant with Mary, her ninth child. He had not wanted too many children either. How could they feed another mouth, all open like baby birds? When she heard about a woman who knew how to get rid of pregnancies, Louise went to see her, nervy with fear. The Indian woman had given her a bitter tea to drink and told her to go straight home.

Louise had just gotten in the house when her stomach began to cramp and burn, as if she'd swallowed fire. Bursting into a sweat, she doubled over clutching her stomach. The pain was so intense she began pacing. Back and forth, from one wall of her musty-smelling house to the other. As she paced, sweating and crying, she became aware of a large Crisco can on the table. A few days before she had filled it with moose lard. Now, without thinking, she pulled off the lid, scooped out a chunk of gray fat with her fingers and shoved it in her mouth.

Back and forth she paced. Crying and shaking, she paced and ate, until the big can was empty.

Maribeth Harper, also known as Mary or Toots, was born April 24, the most beautiful, and for a time, the least confident of Louise's five daughters.

Now, of course, Louise was glad her children were with her. She chuckled when she remembered the time she was ready to give them all away. And Sam, too. That business with her cousin, Helen Callahan. Helen never married, to everyone's mystification. Well, Louise knew why. And so did her husband. After Sam died, Louise, Helen, and Grandma Callahan—who was Helen's mother and Louise's aunt—got together every week to play bridge. Helen, still single because she had never gotten over Sam; Louise, Sam's widow; and Grandma Callahan, all together, playing bridge.

Grandma Callahan, now there was a smart woman. She'd out-foxed that no-good husband of hers, a man Louise wouldn't let her sons go near—that bugger!

Grandma Callahan was the first woman to get a divorce in Fairbanks. Certainly the first Native woman. And she was awarded property, too. She had money rolling in from renting to the hoostitutes. Wasn't her fault the property was in the red-light district. Louise had to admit those dames were good for something. Especially after she saw those swanky flush toilets and running water and felt the steam heat in Grandma Callahan's house. All paid for with hoostitute rent money.

As for Helen and Sam, where had Louise gotten the idea to tell Sam he had to take the children if he left her? From her mother-in-law, Jenny Harper? Sam's mother certainly had problems with Arthur before she left him and married Chief Alexander Williams, a man she later admitted was a lazy, no-account chief.

Louise stabbed at the fabric of her dress with the needle. The hem would be lumpy but at least it would be secure. Jenny was a strong woman, and funny. Louise remembered when Walter bought his mother a brand new pair of white-lady shoes. Red leather, high button top, with high heels. Jenny put them on, teetered a few steps, and nearly fell over. From the aggravated look on that hawk-Indian face of hers, you could see fashion didn't mean a damned thing to her. Walter wasn't even out the door when Jenny took the shoes to the chopping block, picked up an ax and, WHAM, off flew the heels!

Jenny, like Louise's father, John Minook, had the gift of sensing things. A few weeks after Walter married that white nurse in 1918, Jenny wandered down to the river. When she looked out over the flat, gray water crusted with ice, she'd had a bad feeling. Like something dark sidling up to her, she told Louise. Then, a month later, Walter and his bride boarded the ill-fated *Princess Sophia*.

Louise bit off the thread, jabbed the needle into the pincushion and patted the hem flat. The dress was a dark cotton print. Maybe no one would notice if the stitches showed. As she pushed the dress aside to iron later, another memory came unbidden—her mother telling her about her great grandmother.

When the woman was old, about forty-five, weary, and ill, she decided she'd had enough. It was time for the big sleep. So she gave a party for her best friends, serving tea and food and giving each a gift. Moccasins, mittens, a jacket, beads, something of hers. After the guests left the woman's son took her to a shelter he had built on the frozen river. There, alone, she spent her final hours. So simple, Louise thought. Not like now, with doctors hooking you up to all kinds of tubes, dragging life on and on, beating a person almost to death to keep them alive.

Louise sighed. The spirits, like that one at Weese's years before, had no business hanging around. More like a ghost, that one. Playing tricks, wanting attention. Just like a man. Seemed only yesterday Weese called, so scared, her voice shaking when she asked how to get rid of a ghost.

Weese's husband's friend, it was *bootlani* to say his name, had died. Cancer. He'd been ill for more than a year while renting a room upstairs. The noises started after he died. A door closing, a bed creaking. Sounds so soft they could be explained away. The kids and Tex joked, "Get rid of the ghost or oil the hinges!"

At thirty-eight and a solid size twenty, Weese still had traces of the lush sex appeal that had gotten her into trouble in her younger days. She was the fourth of five daughters and the only one with a velvety voice. She also had inherited much of her mother's sensitivity to the spirit world. But this ghost she couldn't handle, she was too afraid. So she called her mother.

Francis dropped Louise off at Weese's on his way to work. Weese poured their coffee and told Louise about the sounds, the crowded feeling in the kitchen, the pain in her hip. Louise thought a moment.

"How long have you heard the noises?" Her voice had deepened over the years and she sounded like a man.

"A few weeks," Weese said. "But it was worse yesterday, Halloween." The tension in her back and neck was giving her a headache.

"Hmmm." Louise looked at the entryway and staircase. "The day the dead walk, that's what Catholics call Halloween." She pushed her chair back and got to her feet. "Help me up the stairs, I want to see his room."

Louise was sixty-one at the time and had a heart condition, arthritis, and glaucoma. Her glasses were so swimmingly thick that when she said she saw something, people looked doubtful. What she meant was to *sense*.

With Weese supporting her, Louise climbed the stairs to what had been the boarder's room. Gray light filtered through a sheer curtain over the window. Unpainted walls were sprinkled with thumbtack holes. A twin bed with a faded plaid spread, an army footlocker, a wobbly floor lamp and a worn chair covered in flowered tapestry crowded the small room. To the left was the closet. The closet door, known to open and shut by itself, was closed.

Louise stood quietly for a long time. Then she turned and they made their way back down stairs. Holding the table for support, she lowered herself into her chair. "Here's what you do," she said, breathing heavily. "Get a fish and cut off the tail. Put the tail up over your door." She pointed at a spot between the ceiling and doorframe.

"A fish tail?" Weese stared at her.

Louise nodded. "To keep bothersome spirits away, spirits who play tricks. And to protect you if someone curses you." Her voice trailed off.

"People with a long sickness . . ." she said, avoiding the man's name.

Weese knew she meant the man who had died of cancer. "When they die, they leave bits of themselves that disturb where they lived." Louise waved a hand around the room, and a chill ran down Weese's back.

Weese drove her mother back to her cabin on Fifth Avenue in the shaky old Ford Tex had won in a card game. Then she went to the grocery store and bought a whitefish. When she got home, she cut off the tail and wrapped it in waxed paper. No use having it smell and attract flies or drip on people's heads. Standing on a chair, she pounded a small nail through the packet into the wall. Pulling the chair back, she surveyed her work. You could hardly see the tail through the paper.

When her daughter Julie came home from school that afternoon, she looked around, puzzled. "What'd you do, Mom? It's different in here." That night, Tex slept without tossing or getting up to pace as he had every night since his friend's death. Over the next few days, the noises from the empty bedroom faded. Even Weese's back and hip pain disappeared. No one noticed the small packet over the door.

◇ ◇ ◇

Louise had been hearing the low, soothing voices for several days. Gentle, caressing voices. Only Weese had a similar voice, low and melodious. But this was not Weese. These voices came when Louise was going to sleep or just waking up. She heard them when no one else was around. She knew they belonged to her ancestors.

One night her chest pains refused to go away when she took her heart medicine. "Where's the pain, Mom?" Weese said, her round face tense.

"Here," Louise pointed to her left side and arm. Her breathing was shallow and her skin looked pasty. George stood by the closet, his Japanese-Indian face young and healthy. She couldn't remember ever seeing him so handsome.

"Let's get you to the hospital!" Weese grabbed her coat and hollered for her son. "Steve, take us to the hospital, you'll be faster than an ambulance!"

"Here, Mom," Weese said. "Can you get your coat around you?" Stooping, Weese pulled off her mother's slippers and shoved on a pair of pile-lined boots. It was July and warm outside, but the older woman's hands and feet were ice-cold.

"George," Louise said, her voice so low Weese wasn't sure she'd heard right. "George, come with me." Weese stared at her mother, but Louise was looking at the closet.

"OK, Mom, I got the car started," Steve said. His young face was pale

Louise holding Flora Jane

under unruly dark hair. Steve, like his brother Jim, was tall and solidly built. Nearly lifting his grandmother, he helped her to the car, while Weese hurried ahead to open the doors.

At the hospital and hooked up to an oxygen tank and monitor, Louise looked at Weese, sitting next to the bed. Beneath the hospital smells, Louise caught a whiff of river air. Like the Yukon in the spring, the green of things growing, the passing smell of snow.

"I saw George by the door . . ." she said, slowly. Her voice was so deep and low, Weese had to lean closer. Louise's short, broad hands rested on the blanket, and she gently rubbed the diamond and opal ring on her finger. The ring George had given her for her birthday years ago. George, her friend and lover after Sam's death. George, who was like a father to her youngest children, and to Mike, her grandson.

When World War II broke out, George had been hauled off to an internment camp in Tanana. Then Francis was captured and spent nearly two years as a prisoner of war in one of those German camps. Stalag something. Louise had been so afraid, but thank the Lord, they'd both come back. She remembered her youngest daughter, Mary, asking, "Why'd you never marry George, Mom?"

"I didn't want to give up the Harper name," she had answered.

◇ ◇ ◇

By the side of the bed, Weese watched her mother, who seemed to have dozed off. After a moment, Louise opened her eyes.

"Bury me in my yellow dress," she said. She could have been ordering groceries. "I don't want black. Don't let anyone wear black to my funeral."

Louise had seen enough black at funerals to last a few lifetimes. The yellow dress was her favorite. More important, it looked good on her.

"OK, Mom," Weese said. She felt her throat close.

"Oh," Louise remembered something else. "I already told Flora Jane, now I'll tell you. Bury me with this ring George gave me. Don't let anyone take it."

Weese nodded. She knew some were eyeing that ring. Well, too bad for them.

"Mom, you're going to be all right. You just needed oxygen." Weese took a breath to keep her voice steady. She worked nights in the emergency room at St. Joseph's Hospital. She knew as much as any nurse when it came to emergency care.

Louise looked beyond her daughter. Near the door, George was smiling. Behind him she saw shadowy lights and shapes, then a glimpse of her mother and father, and Sam and Jenny, and there was Hilda, her first born.

Weese was leaning so close, she should have felt heat from her mother's skin. But there was none. Only the sound of labored breathing. Then she saw her mother's lips move.

"George is here, Weese . . . they all are."

Epilogue

Flora Jane, Connie with baby Tommy, and Bertha Schafer

In 1949, we were living on Tudor road in Anchorage in a house Dad had built. Snowdrifts could reach ten to fifteen feet overnight when the wind was fierce. It seemed we were constantly snowed in—Dad having to shovel us out, sometimes all the way to Seward highway. A neighbor with a rented tractor occasionally offered to help, but we seldom had money to chip in and Dad didn't want to be "beholden."

In those days, my grandmother, Louise Harper, came on the train from Fairbanks to visit us—Aunt Elsie usually sent her a ticket since Oscar worked for the railroad. Grandma was a short, round woman with dark skin and hair, and she looked cuddly, like a doll or teddy bear. I never cuddled her—just a quick hug, if that. None of our family cuddled, we hardly touched.

When I was six, Grandma was fifty-seven, partly deaf, and her English, in

Wrangell Institute

a deep, low voice, was hard to understand. I was too shy to talk, but I'll never forget the way Mom and Aunt Elsie hovered around her. During those visits, they talked and laughed at some bit of gossip, sharing memories none of the rest of us had. As if they were from a different country—and only together could they be who they had been.

During these visits, Grandma stayed with Elsie and Oscar in their small, tar-papered house. Their house seemed bigger than ours because it had a real bedroom in the basement. One I'd never seen because of the rats.

After Mom went back to work, first at Snow White Laundry, then at the Loussac Library, she'd send Grandma twenty-five to forty dollars a month, depending on what we could afford, which wasn't much in the 1950s.

When I was a freshman in high school, Grandma stayed with me when my parents drove to Missouri to visit Dad's family. I was giddy over not having parents bird-dog me for two weeks and forgot the stew Dad left in the freezer. I was to heat it for our dinners. Instead, Grandma and I ate soup and crackers, clearing out an entire three-shelf cupboard of Campbells, hoarded in event of disaster. Dad told me I could keep the money saved from groceries. So I didn't buy much, not even bread, which, as everyone knew, made you fat. During the day while I was in school, however, Grandma would hike over the bumpy path to Elsie's house and eat up, muttering, "There's nothing to eat over there."

In 1965, I was student-teaching at East Anchorage High School when I

EPILOGUE

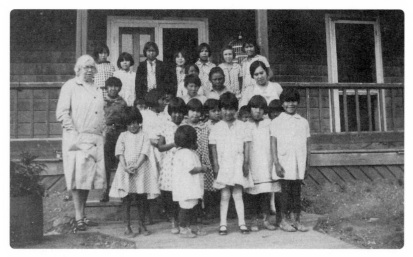

Mrs. Call (left), a friend and mentor to Flora Jane Harper, standing in front of the Tanana orphanage.

visited Grandma at the Alaska Native Service Hospital. She was recovering from cataract surgery and she peered at me through thick glasses. As soon as I sat down, her lunch tray arrived, delivered by a harried attendant. The vaguely metallic smell of institutional food filled the room. On a brown tray, a large white plate held roast beef, mashed potatoes with gravy, canned peas and carrots, two slices of white bread and hard pats of margarine. Green Jell-O and a pot of tea stood off to the side. I steered Grandma's groping hand to the fork and watched as she tried to cut the meat she couldn't see. Finally, she picked up the bread.

As we talked—me shouting—I cut the beef, scooped up some peas, carrots and mashed potatoes and fed her. In the halls, I heard the nurses and attendants dashing around, pushing carts, delivering meals, medications, answering phones. Busy, busy. So who helped Grandma eat when she had no visitors?

"How's she supposed to get well if she can't see to eat anything besides bread?" I raged to my parents that evening.

Mom enjoyed talking about her childhood. How Grandma could whistle for the wind and make breezes appear. How at fish camp, oil from fish hanging overhead dripped on her as she stoked the smudge fires. She was five years old, and that was her job. "My cloth parka was so stiff with fish oil, it stood up by itself when I took it off," she said. "I stank of fish all summer, my hair, my clothes . . . I couldn't get rid of the smell."

Grandma taught herself to read and write, learning from movie magazines. When she moved on to *Look* and *Collier's*, she disdained the movie magazines, calling them "trash."

I heard about Mom's Chemawa days, and Eklutna, and Wrangell. I knew how much she loved teaching. When I was older she told me about Bonner. His letters were in our attic. Dad had seen them. "Oh, your father," Mom said, laughter glinting in her eyes. "He's had his share . . . he understands." The letters were forgotten, along with my doll Penny, when the house was sold.

By the time I reached high school, I was caught up in boys, clothes, *Vogue* magazine, the idea of New York, and leaving Alaska. I wanted to travel the world, write for *Time* magazine, wear a trenchcoat, smoke, and look sultry while waiting in the rain for a midnight plane.

I graduated from the University of Alaska Fairbanks, the only college Mom and Dad would help pay for, and taught home economics at Elmendorf AFB. In 1968 when I was twenty-four, I married an Army Lieutenant. *"You can get married now . . . I don't want you to be an old maid like I was,"* Mom was always saying. It was January 19, and forty below on our wedding day. Dad's camera froze and my orchids turned brown. Our tiny wedding was followed by a brunch at the Captain Cook hotel. Photographs from the thawed camera show us smiling under a large chunk of wood torn from Cook's ship, *Resolution*.

In 1971, under the haze of shredded emotions and divorce, I left Alaska for Honolulu—choosing Hawaii so no one would feel sorry for me. Mom was devastated. Years later, when I saw some of her Eklutna photographs, I understood why. My young husband resembled Bonner. While she cried and Dad raged over their only child getting a divorce and leaving Alaska, I was grateful for Aunt Elsie's quiet sympathy. In 1974, I moved to San Francisco.

My mother retired in 1972. She had worked as a library assistant at the Loussac Library for nineteen years. She was such a fixture, the mayor and city council gave her a retirement luncheon, some of which was televised on Channel 2. In 1974, Dad talked her into leaving Alaska for Sequim, Washington, so they "could stop worrying about pipes freezing and scraping ice and snow off windshields."

By 1990, I was remarried and living in the San Francisco Bay Area. In August that year Dad died in his sleep. I flew to Sequim.

"When I couldn't wake him," Mom told me, her face pale, her voice shaking, "I hit him and hit him with my fists! 'You bastard,' I yelled, 'you weren't supposed to go before me.'"

Her grief filled the house. Unable to sleep at night, she walked up

EPILOGUE

Mary Denton and family

Tom and Connie Paddock

and down the thirty-foot hall that ran the length of the house. In the small bedroom where Dad died, I listened to her pace. One night I sat up and tried to meditate. Gradually, I became aware of something around me. After a moment, I felt hands, as if my head and shoulders were being covered with a blanket, or a cape, gray and hooded. The hood had a bill, like a baseball cap, but long and pointed. I was scared stiff. Then I felt Grandma's presence.

Things did not get easier for us right away. Mom's depression and physical pain fueled her misery into bitter words.

Over the next several months, Aunt Weese (sober for several years) stayed with Mom when I couldn't. Weese's calm presence deflected a lot of Mom's anxiety and tension, allowing us some light-hearted moments and a wonderful relationship at the end. It was the first time I'd been around Weese. I laughed at her quick, dry wit, and hung on her words when she talked about spirits and Grandma.

"Keep on writing," Mom said, the last time I saw her. She was resting in bed, propped up with four pillows and she had a bird's-eye view of my mouth. "And take care of your teeth," she added, critically admiring my dental work.

"Who'd a thought, huh," she said later, her eyes growing distant. I laughed, remembering. "Who'd a thought" in our family always prefaced a reminiscence—usually over how far "a little ol' Indian"—as Mom called herself—had come. Yet I know in the end, her spirit would return to the headwaters of the Yukon. As our ancestors had promised.

John and Don Harper around 1985–1990   *Elsie and Flora at Chemawa reunion 1980*

Mary, Connie and Don, around 1990–1995

Author's Afterword

Elsie and Oscar Fast had three children—Phyllis, Richard, and Esther—whom I once bossed around. After Oscar's death, Elsie bought, rented, and sold property. She eventually traveled to South America, Mexico, Hawaii, and Paris, where Phyllis attended the Sorbonne

John Harper and his wife, Isabel, had one daughter, Johanna. John worked for Nerland's Home Furnishing in Fairbanks until his retirement. Once I asked him about his years at Chemawa and he grimaced. "Oh, that was awful," he said, adding so many swear words I never mentioned it again.

Don, the youngest Harper, married a Native woman from Sitka and had a daughter, Robin. Don worked as an electrician until his retirement.

Mary, or Toots as friends knew her, married Ashley Denton of Georgia where they have several hundred acres of tobacco farmland. They have seven children— Lloyd, Bruce, Max (deceased), Robert, Elizabeth, Debra and Dana. Mary absorbed the South to the extent that her charming Georgia accent made her unintelligible to relatives. Nonetheless, we found ourselves stretching our words and adding syllables here and there after every visit south.

Connie graduated from Haskell Institute in Kansas and served as chief clerk for the Alaska House of Representatives from 1962 to 1974. She later served on the board of directors for the Tenakee Springs Village Corporation. She married a Tlingit Indian, Tom Paddock, a bridge-builder who lived in Juneau, and they had three children— Maxine, Tom, and Anna Louise.

Arthur worked for Fairbanks businessman Maxey Miller as a mechanic and driver. Art married an Athabascan woman, Angela, and they had three children— Edward, Ronald, and Joyce.

Francis, a POW during the Second World War, graduated from the University of Washington and worked for the Boeing Company in Seattle. He died after a heart attack while skiing at Wounded Knee, South Dakota. He and Nancy had no children.

Weese was an admitting clerk in ER at Fairbanks Memorial Hospital until her retirement. Many of her ten children—Mike, Susan, Julie, James, Steve, Ella, Kathy, Diane, Nichole, and Sherry—and grandchildren live in Alaska. Like her mother, Louise, Weese could sense the presence of spirits. "They don't bother me," she told me.

Walt, the son cursed by the *deeyninh*, fell in forbidden love with his second cousin. An alcoholic, he lived on the streets of Anchorage and Fairbanks, refusing all help. He surprised everyone by outliving many of his siblings and spent his final days in the Sitka Pioneers' Home.

* * *

The hardscrabble life of Sam and Louise and their ten children gave way to improved opportunities for their twenty-nine grandchildren. Many have technical training or college degrees. Some have their own businesses. I apologize that the following is only a partial list. It also does not include the achievements of Louise's great grandchildren

Kathy Blair, Weese's daughter, was deputy director for the Fairbanks Native Association. She lives in Fairbanks and has a son and a daughter.

Mike Harper, Weese's firstborn, who lived with his grandmother, Louise, was an aide to Alaska Governor Jay Hammond in the 1970s. Later, Mike was president of the Kuskokwim Corporation in Anchorage. He and his wife, Jane, have a daughter.

Phyllis Fast, Elsie's oldest daughter, owned and managed a computer business with her sister, Esther. In 1998, Phyllis earned a PhD in anthropology from Harvard University. Today, Professor Fast teaches at the University of Alaska Anchorage.

Richard Fast, Elsie's son, consulted with the State of Alaska in Juneau to help the visually impaired, until his retirement. He now lives in Anchorage.

Esther Fast, Elsie's youngest daughter, has two daughters and works in insurance in Anchorage.

Johanna Harper, John's daughter, lives in Anchorage and works for CIRI, a Native corporation. She has a son and daughter.

Maxine Paddock Richert, Connie's oldest daughter, was the corporate secretary for Sealaska, a regional Native corporation in Juneau until her retirement. She and her husband have a son and daughter.

Beth Denton, Mary's oldest daughter ran her own printing business and now works out of Atlanta.

Debra Denton, Mary's second daughter, has her own interior design business in Georgia.

Lloyd, Mary's oldest son, was a switchman for CSX Railroad until his retirement.

Bruce, Mary's second oldest son, works for the Georgia Department of Corrections.

Bobby, Mary's youngest son, is an engineer for CSX Railroad in Georgia.

Jan (Petri) Harper Haines, Flora Jane's daughter, taught at Orion Junior High on Elmendorf Air Force Base. She later worked in advertising and marketing in Honolulu and San Francisco. She now writes fulltime and this is her first book.

* * *

In 1994, the University of Alaska Fairbanks rededicated a building the Harper Building in honor of Flora Jane Harper Petri.

Reader's Group Questions

1. Why did Louise run from an arranged marriage that would have benefited her family? Do you think she had conflicting feelings about her decision? Did her father?

2. What were the "games" Louise played with her children?

3. What role did the red-light district play in the education of the four older Harper children?

4. Did Sam Harper make the right decision sending his four oldest children to the Oregon boarding school? What were his options? How did the six younger children feel when the four oldest returned after ten years?

5. What inspired Flora Jane's ambition to teach? What role models did she have? What helped her pursue her dream despite illness, poverty, and the racism she encountered?

6. How did Louise's alcoholism affect her family? How did her children cope? How do you think race and racism impact alcoholism for Alaska Natives?

7. Why did Flora Jane reject Professor Geist's marriage proposal? Why do you think he phrased the proposal the way he did? What does this say about

the opportunities for Native women at the time?

8. Forgiveness and love seem to play an important part in Flora Jane's life. Years after her white lover had left her for a white woman, what was his reaction upon Flora Jane with her child? How did she feel?

9. Do you think Jenny Harper was right in allowing her husband Arthur Harper to believe Walter wasn't his son? Why did she do it? Was Walter better off for having remained in Alaska? What would he have missed if he had left?

10. How did Francis manage to keep his sanity while a POW in World War II? How did he heal from the shock of those years? What role did Doreen play and why was she so bitter when he married Nancy?

11. Which stories resonated the most for you? If you were to write a play based on one scene, which would you choose?

12. When something unusual happened in nature, Athabascans believed something unusual was coming to the people. Do you think such incidents are a coincidence or based in fact?

About the Author

J an (Petri) Harper Haines was born in Sitka, Alaska of Athabascan, Irish, Russian, and Dutch descent.

In 1990, she began gathering oral histories about her mother and grandmother's lives on the Yukon River. This family memoir grew out of those early stories. Jan earned a bachelor's degree from the University of Alaska-Fairbanks, where her mother, Flora Jane Harper, was the University's first Alaska Native woman to graduate in 1935.

The author's short stories have appeared in magazines and literary publications.

Jan is a former secondary education teacher and has also had a twenty-year career in advertising and marketing in Honolulu and San Francisco. She lives in Marin County, California with her husband, Larry, an architect.

For more information visit www.harperhaines.com.